CHI-RYU JIUJITSU

Energy Way of Gentle Technique

By Dan Popp

With

Isham Latimer / John Costanzo / John McDonald

www.wakinghands.com

Copyright © 2023 by Dan Popp

Kanji / front cover: Chi-Ryu Jiujitsu
Brushed by the author (2014)

All rights reserved. No part of this book may be reproduced in any form or by any means, electronic or mechanical, including photocopying, recording, or by any information storage and retrieval system, without permission in writing from the author and Kamel Press.

Printed in the United States of America

PHOTO CREDITS

See Appendix

Proudly Published by Kamel Press, LLC.
Visit www.KamelPress.com/Popp for more from this author!

Library of Congress Control Number: 2022951273

ISBN-13:

978-1-62487-068-2 – paperback
978-1-62487- 069-9 – ebook

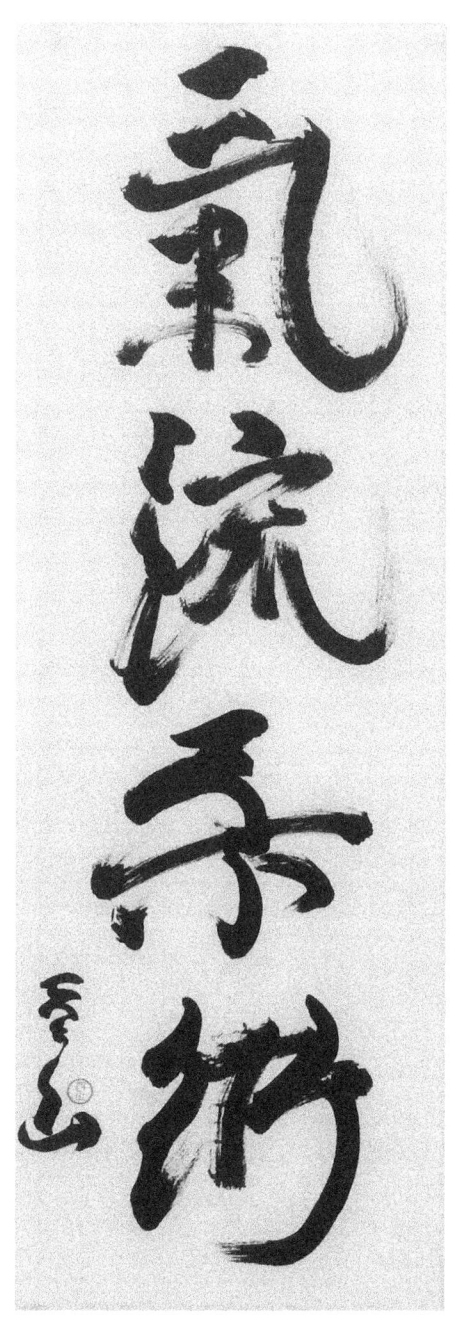

Chi-Ryu Jiujitsu

Brushed by the author - 2014

BREATH
The Spirit of a Warrior

It is found in the way that he or she forges ahead
despite the many challenges they encounter in life.

For even in the straightness of their sword, staff or spear;
they have seen the bends, splinters, and notches,
which they accept and embrace in their desire
to become one with the true spirit of their tools/weapons.

He or she must guard against those who through envy,
admiration, greed, and self-hate try to sabotage their missions,
and convince them that their tools/weapons are imperfect.

The true warrior knows that there is no such thing as imperfection,
but that truth and love are woven into one and becomes
lifeline of the true warrior.

The definition of truth and love is not separate from the aspects of life and death.

It is as the true spirit of the wave is found in its rising and falling.

The cloth is defined by its folds as well as in its flatness.

The road is defined by the turns as well as in its straightness.

Truth is found in the experience of hurt, as well as in that of joy.

To transcend self-righteousness is to become as a warrior accepting truth in spirit.

Grandmaster Isham Latimer
– June 2017 –

DEDICATION

The art of Chi-Ryu Jiujitsu is dedicated to the following individuals without whose teachings and guidance the originators of Chi-Ryu Jiujitsu would not have been able to develop this style.

In chronological order:

Sensei Joe Drual

Grandmaster Latimer's first karate sensei. He was a very thorough and inspiring instructor, as well as a very accomplished martial artist in both Isshinryu Karate and Seiryoku Jujutsu.

Makakuvu Ali El Bey

Shared Sanuces-Ryu Jiujitsu technique with Grandmaster Latimer.

Master Malachi Lee

Master Lee's knowledge, skill, philosophy and patience instilled in us our passion and love of the martial arts.

Grandmaster Toby Cooling

Grandmaster Cooling urged us to continue investigating the depth of knowledge provided by the martial arts and to "Go out and gain new knowledge and bring it back to the Order of Isshin-Ryu."

Master Aston Hugh

Master Hugh gave us the gift of Hsing-I Liu Ho Bafa Chuan.

AUTHOR'S DEDICATION

To my instructors:

Grandmaster Isham Latimer / Chi-Ryu Jiujitsu

Grandmaster Rick Manglinong / SMP Arnis

Master Dave Joyner / Kendo

In memory of my sensei in Isshin-Ryu karate:

Grandmaster Toby Cooling (1944 – 2022) / Order of Isshin-Ryu Karate

"I have come to the frightening conclusion that I am the decisive element. It is my personal approach that creates the climate. It is my daily mood that makes the weather. I possess tremendous power to make life miserable or joyous. I can be a tool of torture or an instrument of inspiration, I can humiliate or humor, hurt or heal. In all situations, it is my response that decides whether a crisis is escalated or de-escalated, and a person is humanized or de-humanized. If we treat people as they are, we make them worse. If we treat people as they ought to be, we help them to become what they are capable of becoming."

--Johann Wolfgang von Goethe

ACKNOWLEDGEMENTS

Thank you to the Three Pillars of Chi-Ryu Jiujitsu: Grandmaster Isham Latimer, Master John Costanzo, and Master John McDonald. These men created and formally founded a unique system of martial arts that can be studied and practiced for a lifetime. I am honored to memorialize your system with this publication. Most importantly, I treasure the fact I call you my brothers.

To the various students of Chi-Ryu Jiujitsu who provided invaluable contributions to the effort behind this book. Harold Townsend has documented many of the forms of Chi-Ryu Jiujitsu and unselfishly provided his personal notes to assist with narrative behind the techniques. Joshua Poventud categorized the various movements and authored the original explanations of each movement. Bryce Kadash worked tirelessly with the Three Pillars and myself in recent years to help us hone in on the applications to present in this publication.

Special thanks to Master Aston Hugh, who gave the Three Pillars the gift of Hsing-I Liuhebafa Chuan. This art is fascinating and incredible to practice and is deeply embedded into the roots of all martial arts of today.

My respects always for each of my martial arts instructors: Grandmaster Rick Manglinong (Kombatan, Modern Arnis), Grandmaster Isham Latimer (Chi-Ryu Jiujitsu), and Sensei Dave Joyner (Kendo). Your lessons and examples continue to serve as my motivation and guide along the path of self-improvement.

Special acknowledgement to my late sensei, Grandmaster Toby Cooling, who passed February 2022. Your example and guidance will continue to serve as a compass for my martial arts career. All of my trips to see my sensei at his home and spend time with him provided much more than martial arts instruction. Those will be memories I'll cherish the rest of my life and, hopefully, can pass along to others to enrich their lives as you did for me.

Thank you to those providing a Foreword to this publication…Masters Jesus Jimenez, Diane Ortenzio-Cooling, Carl Martin, Denny Shaffer, and Willie Wilson. We are humbled immensely by your contribution to this project.

To my parents Frank and Carol Popp. Thanks for your total support regarding all of my efforts both professional and personal.

To my wonderful daughters, Britteni and Kayla. I know you are my biggest supporters… and I am both your biggest fan. Keep working towards your own goals in life and, no matter what, I'll be the proudest father ever!

The Kamel Press team, as usual, is amazing to work with. Once again, you've exceeded my expectations.

Thank you to Master John Costanzo for the design of the front and back covers. I was not exactly the easiest 'client' to deal with, but you kept your wits and got this thing to the finish line!

Special thanks to Greg LeBlanc for providing the tribute graphic of Grandmaster Toby Cooling. Greg is a black belt member of the Trappe, MD dojo of the Order of Isshin-Ryu and serves as the Information Officer for the OI. Thank you sir for all that you do!

And finally, all credit goes to my savior, Jesus Christ.

TABLE OF CONTENTS

Foreword 1

Introduction 5

Chapter 1 - The Three Pillars of Chi-Ryu Jiujitsu 9

Chapter 2 - Systems Forming Chi-Ryu Jiujitsu 25

Chapter 3 - Development of Chi-Ryu Jiujitsu 37

Chapter 4 - Breathing Exercises 43

Chapter 5 - MiXXiNG 71

Chapter 6 - Movements of Chi-Ryu Jiujitsu 81

Chapter 7 - Liuhebafa 119

Chapter 8 - Forms of Chi-Ryu Jiujitsu 141

Chapter 9 - Raking Fist Form 145

Chapter 10 - Breaking Waves Form 165

Chapter 11 - Waking Dragon Form 183

Appendix: Photo Credits 198

Sources 199

About the Author 202

FOREWORD

"*Nothing is, until it is.*" This is a short expression that refers to the causes, effects, and consequences of all our actions. Every act we do has that effect. Without a doubt, the creation of a martial art style is included within that simple expression. With detail, care and passion, Dan Popp presents in this book the essence of Chi-Ryu Jiujitsu, a style of martial arts set up by Grandmaster Isham Latimer with the close collaboration of Master John Costanzo and Master John McDonald. In this book the reader will not only find an interesting and revealing reading but will feel the interest of deeply studying the notions that are the foundations of Chi-Ryu Jiujitsu that can applied to all aspects of life by practitioners or non-practitioners of martial arts.

Each style of martial arts contains two basic aspects; one is strictly martial, and the other is philosophical in nature. Chi-Ryu Jiujitsu is not the exception to that maxim. Reading this book made me remember what Jose Díaz described as "*Each technique has to be executed with finesse and aggressiveness*" and Aston Hugh as "*Everything in life has a rhythm, you just have to find it.*"[1] To understand those words, we cannot preclude the study of the past to understand the present.

The founder of a martial art style gave his personal view of a series of techniques. When practicing a style, we repeat that version. The importance of a martial art style is to lead the student to be able to advance his or her leadership qualities such as: loyalty, courage, desire, physical stamina, empathy, emotional stamina, decisiveness, timing, competitiveness, self-confidence, accountability, credibility, tenacity, and dependability. Once the student has reached that maturity and becomes his own *sensei*, then the seed for creating a style will be eager to germinate. Not everybody can be a leader and not everyone has an interest in creating a style.

Chi-Ryu Jiujitsu demonstrates the great responsibility, seriousness, and optimism of Grandmaster Isham Latimer, Master John Costanzo and Master John McDonald. Throughout this book, the three pillars of Chi-Ryu Jiujitsu reveal their techniques that, based on their experiences, certainly work out in a world that is increasingly violent.

Master Jesus M. Jiménez
9th dan - Order of Isshin-Ryu Martial Arts
Sunsu Dojo

---

[1] Both were black belts from the New York dojo of the Order of Isshin-Ryu system.

After reading the first three chapters of Chi-Ryu Jiujitsu – The Energy Way of Gentle Technique, I was inspired and excited to see this masterpiece of work, a lifetime commitment to establish a new system of martial arts. Grandmaster Latimer's dream of combining the core principles of Isshin-Ryu Karate with some core principles of other martial arts systems, has led him to develop the Chi-Ryu Jiujitsu system. This combination of works has helped him create this new flowing system by applying core movements to make it *Mushin*, or "mind of no-mind."

I commend the efforts of Grandmaster Latimer for taking his dream, making it a reality, and collaborating with Master John Constanzo and Master John McDonald to establish this new system. These men have dedicated a large amount of their lives, time, and committed effort to make this system applicable.

This book is a must read for all Martial Artists who have the ambition to be great in their own systems.

Master Carl Martin, Hanshi
9th dan - Isshin-Ryu Karate-do
TOKI-Dojo

Everything must evolve or perish. Very few things survive intact over long periods of time. It was something my late husband, Hanshi Walter Cooling, believed and prepared for. Criminals continually share, compare, and hone their skills to overcome the defenses of law enforcement and citizens. We, too, must do the same to maintain an advantage over criminals and evildoers.

When it comes to martial arts, there are two types of practitioners: replicators and innovators. Those are terms coined by the illustrious author and martial artist, W. Hock Hochheim. A replicator is one who follows exactly what they were taught by their instructor, with little to no thought or addition by the person themselves. By contrast, an innovator is one who takes the knowledge gained from their instructors and adds their own experiences and refinements, along with updates to counter whatever maneuvers criminals may design.

With Chi Ryu Jujitsu, you have three innovators who have done just that. This book will be your introduction to the concepts and paths they developed, but if you really want to feel the depth of this art, find the time and train with them. You won't be disappointed.

Master Diane Ortenzio-Cooling
9th dan, Order of Isshin-Ryu Martial Arts
7th dan (Dayang Pito), Sining Marsiyal ng Pilipinas Arnis

I am honored to say a few words about my friend, colleague, and Red Dragon Tab Brother – Grandmaster Isham Latimer. Regarding the latter, the Red Dragon Tab award is given by a 100% vote from the black belt instructors of my dojo. It is based on our collective selection of someone with impeccable credentials as a martial artist, leader, and mentor to our dojo. You must have a 100% vote to receive the award.

I met Grandmaster Latimer after his annual seminar, demonstrating his own system he had created, *Chi-Ryu Jiujitsu*, in tandem with his main students who co-developed the system, Master John Costanzo and Master John McDonald. I was both impressed and inspired. Later, I sought him out to help me develop a better understanding, and across the board equitable culture, for both Caucasian and African American students. It indeed was the right advice he provided.

The accomplishments of the Red Dragon students are a matter of record. Some years later, I developed my own martial arts system. Once again, due to the example of Grandmaster Latimer. He is a well spring of knowledge and can do everything he teaches and demonstrates. Some have discovered that the hard way.

Thank you, dear friend. I look forward to your book and continuing to glean more of your rock-solid advice and knowledge.

Grandmaster Denny Shaffer
10th dan – Founder, Red Dragon Sen I Jutsu
10th dan – Isshinryu Karate
1st dan – Kung Fu
1st dan – Half Circle Jiujitsu
1st kyu – Wado Ryu Karate
Founder, Strike Back Street Defense

When I was contacted by Grandmaster Isham A. Latimer to write a foreword for the publication of *Chi-Ryu Jiujitsu: Energy Way of Gentle Technique*, I told him it would be an honor to read his manuscript and his work describing his journey in Martial Arts. Once I received the draft pages, I immediately opened the manuscript and sat down to read until I finished the last page. Page after page I was filled with a familiar sense of recognition and thought, "I am talking to myself." The same people, the same systems, and the way he trains with Master John Costanzo and Master John McDonald which make up the *Three Pillars*, filled the spirit of martial arts deeply embedded in our lives, reminded me of my own organization - Karate Five.

This book burrows deeply into the training, philosophy, and mental acumen required if one is to achieve the martial arts level this book describes. Sensei Latimer's techniques are taken from a true martial artist's heart which is not about "pretenders" but describes all the ingredients to create a single togetherness as a unique art in and of itself requiring mental, physical and emotional synergy to master at the level at which he and his students have arrived.

The day his manuscript arrived had been chaotic as I faced a gridlock of deadlines but when I slipped into the pages of his book and started reading I just wanted to know more and how his masterful technique related to my decades of training as well as anyone else with a sincere desire for this art who wants to grow and master this unique art form. Chi-Ryu Jiujitsu is a complete system that has been driven and tested by collaboration of all three masters. They've taken their indisputable decades of knowledge and put together a complete system, which is no easy undertaking, and created a complete; yet unchallengeable system that can stand firmly on its own.

As I mentally stepped back across the span of decades I've known Grandmaster Latimer and contemplated a deeper look into the approach of Chi-Ryu Jiujitsu; I understand how they used the AVVC approaches that are actual moves, variable moves, vision and creativity—so clearly awesome in its creative fusion. Only a martial artist of this caliber to clearly see once you have the *actual move;* then where are my *variable moves;* then when this is done, here comes *the vision* that leads you to *creativity.* All these approaches that the three pillars have put together and ultimately and unequivocally, we call this AVVC process "you" - you then own your art. My concept is this: to *make a difference,* you have to *be a difference* to *see a difference* to know *you made a difference* and for you, Chi-Ryu Jiujitsu *will make that difference.*

All the years and martial arts background of the three pillars combined; one could say, What took you so long to put dreams into reality so others can also enjoy a better understanding of the journey? But understanding the real world of martial arts is nowhere as easy as one might assume; it is not just a physical mastering but mental and emotional as well and without any doubt, their journey has proven this. Any advanced student in Martial Arts can learn and advance in this system. He has taken out the *"roll block"* to allow you to roll your journey to any level you want to achieve.

In my own words to my friend and true martial arts warrior, I would like to say congratulations to Grandmaster Isham Latimer and your co-developers for putting all this AVVC together to create another system of martial arts that works and willingness to boldly share *Chi-Ryu Jiujitsu: Energy Way of Gentle Technique* with others.

Grandmaster Willie Garfield Wilson
10th dan - Isshinryu Karate-do
Karate Five Dojos

INTRODUCTION

Chi-Ryu Jiujitsu is a system of martial arts that has been under development for well over 20 years. Grandmaster Isham Latimer, Master John Costanzo, and Master John McDonald – known as The Three Pillars of Chi-Ryu Jiujitsu - forged through trial and error, blood and sweat to develop this highly effective system. All three men utilized the creativity of their artistic backgrounds to formulate their training methods. Chi-Ryu Jiujitsu is a system that has practicality for street defense as well as maintaining health and flexibility in mind, body, and spirit.

The Three Pillars are martial artists in the broadest sense. They are continually exploring, testing, researching, and evolving their techniques and understanding of what the martial arts has to offer the practitioner. Their intent has always been to add to their training curriculum in order to become complete and well-rounded martial artists. To improve your skill sets as a martial artist requires exposure to many styles of the fighting arts. This continual exploration into various styles and systems is paramount to those looking to move the needle and advance the budo, or the way of the warrior. As I noted in my previous book *Order of Isshin-Ryu: One Family, One Dojo*, "Master Tatsuo Shimabuku began his study of these weapons [Kobudo] in 1959 at the age of 50[2], several years after the official formulation of Isshin-Ryu. He had mastered both Shorin-ryu and Goju-ryu and was one of the highest sought after instructors on the island [Okinawa] at that time, yet he was humble enough to begin training in another system of martial arts called Kobudo. Clearly, Tatsuo Shimabuku continuously searched for a variety of techniques to complement and blend with his Isshin-Ryu system. As all true martial artists do, he was continuously exploring and seeking to expand his capabilities and skills." The author of *Shotokan's Secrets*, Bruce Clayton, Ph.D., also makes this point in his publication, "The old masters were completely different from their modern followers. A master might [create] a karate organization, but he would never join one. The real masters of karate were Okinawans who studied many arts with many teachers. They moved freely from one teacher to another, cherry-picking the techniques and skills that they thought useful."

One of the objectives of Chi-Ryu Jiujitsu is allowing those advanced in years to continue training and exploring the various aspects of the martial arts, due in large part to the tenets of Tai Chi Chuan and how that form of martial arts is practiced. Tai Chi emphasizes the internal aspects of development. Da Liu's book *T'ai Chi Ch'uan and I Ching* points out these various points of reference for importance to the Tai Chi practitioner: mind, breathing, blood circulation, smoothness, balance, centering, relaxation, continuity, coordination, slowness, and effortlessness. Even though development of a strong punch, kick, knee strike, or elbow is an essential element of modern self-defense, those techniques are not solely dependent on strength of muscle alone. The famous karate master Chojun Miyagi was influenced heavily by

---

2 https://en.wikipedia.org/wiki/Isshin-ry%C5%AB

the internal aspects of the Chinese systems as well. He named his system Goju-Ryu after reading in the *Bubishi*, "Inhaling represents softness while exhaling characterizes hardness." Clearly, Miyagi understood the effectiveness of combining the elements of softness and hardness to become a well-rounded martial artist.

As martial artists grow older, on average they tend to slow down in their training or stop training altogether. This could be due in large part to the wear and tear on the body's joints from punching and kicking with full force, snap and power. This type of continuous strain on the body can create irreversible damage as many practitioners end up over time with arthritic problems, or worse, a knee or hip replacement. Grandmaster Latimer has noted that friends from the old days training in judo and jiujitsu have ended up in wheelchairs stemming from the force of techniques practiced over and over again. Surely, strong and forceful basics must be developed in order to understand how to make any given technique effective. However, at what price? As author C.W. Nicol relates in his book *Moving Zen*, "The masters of Tai Chi Chuan are usually advanced in years. Despite advancing years, a person can improve skill and power. Westerners often see something like this and scoff – yet how many men of forty in the West are active in a physical sport? How many men of fifty are active? Sixty? Seventy?" The founders of Chi-Ryu Jujitsu are proponents of moderation when it comes to execution of technique. Develop strength in your technique, but over time also include the benefits of proper breathing and controlled use of your internal energy to heighten the effectiveness of your movements.

The Three Pillars of Chi-Ryu Jiujitsu continue to train together for five hours every Sunday, continually honing their skills and the art they have formulated. They are living proof of how their system can allow a martial artist to continue training well beyond 30 or 40 years in the martial arts.

Chi-Ryu Jiujitsu looks to develop more fully the overall spirit of the person through the practice Chi-Ryu Jiujitsu techniques, breathing, and forms taught within the system. There comes a time in the martial artists' development where attention and focus must be given to developing the overall spirit. This is called *chi* in Chinese and *ki* in Japanese. As Nicol further expresses in his book, "The martial artist must regard his body as a splendid tool for the spirit to use. The body should not be allowed to dominate the spirit." This spirit is developed through continued efforts to train the mind, to become calm and accepting of everything that comes your way and deal with them with fluid effort. The mind is used to keep the purpose of your training at the core of your thoughts and efforts. In the book *Mindful Running*, author Mackenzie Havey tells of distance runner Deena Kastor's experiences. Kastor explains, "Being mindful and paying attention to the things like my form, my breath, and my purpose for each run makes the process of training so much more worthwhile and fulfilling, but also more productive." The student of Chi-Ryu Jiujitsu approaches training the same way, each workout is for the purpose of development of mind and breath, which heightens awareness and productivity as a martial artist.

This introductory volume explains the art of Chi-Ryu Jiujitsu. The founders of this system, called the Three Pillars of Chi-Ryu Jiujitsu, are presented along with the motivation behind the creation of this art. Subsequent chapters provide step-by-step photographs of Chi-Ryu Jiujitsu's basic movements as well as the first several forms which Chi-Ryu Jiujitsu students learn. In addition, the foundation of this system is outlined with the concepts of proper breathing and an exercise unique to Chi-Ryu Jiujitsu called *MiXXiNG* that is the basis of all movement within the system.

Dan Popp
May 30, 2022
Harrisburg, Pennsylvania

THE THREE PILLARS OF CHI-RYU JIUJITSU

CHAPTER 1

"Behind every shadow there is light."
- Grandmaster Isham Latimer

May 2022 - Three Pillars of Chi-Ryu Jiujitsu. L-R: Master John McDonald, Grandmaster Isham Latimer, Master John Costanzo

The founding of Chi-Ryu Jiujitsu involved the combined effort of three martial artists: Grandmaster Isham Latimer, Master John Costanzo, and Master John McDonald. Referred to as the "Three Pillars of Chi-Ryu Jiujitsu," all three men have combined over 120 years of experience in martial arts training consisting of a variety of styles and systems. Grandmaster Latimer had the vision to create a system of martial arts that allowed for freedom of movement and not rely upon sheer muscular strength to defend yourself. Masters Costanzo and McDonald are co-developers of this system, bringing with them diverse and rich backgrounds that enhanced the creative process. These collaborative efforts took place over the past 30 years through much trial and error coupled with serious discussions concerning the most tactically sound techniques and movements. I have been a personal witness to this process for the past 15 years, traveling back and forth from Pennsylvania to New York and New Jersey witnessing first hand the dynamics of all three men. Chi-Ryu Jiujitsu, or CRJ, has emerged from countless hours of experimentation coupled with sound principles learned from existing systems.

All three men bring fascinating backgrounds to the table within the martial arts world. Each man is highly respected for not only their contributions to martial arts but also in their respective professions, as you will see in their individual biographies presented later in this chapter. What is also unique and interesting is that these men all have artistic backgrounds as well. To formulate a system of martial arts certainly requires practical usage of tried and true techniques and movements, which Chi-Ryu Jiujitsu certainly provides. However, a large degree of artistic ability and creativity is also arguably needed to have the vision, motivation, and confidence to take on the immense pressure of developing your own system of martial arts and having the ability to prove its effectiveness. The Three Pillars have this creativity and artistic ability in abundance. Grandmaster Latimer is a painter and musician, Master Costanzo is a graphic designer, and Master McDonald is an actor and acting coach.

Another quality all three men possess is the desire to continually research and seek new knowledge beyond their current sphere of influence. The Japanese refer to this mindset as *shoshin*, or beginner mind, meaning to continually think of yourself as a beginner in order to have an open mind to explore and try new things. In the book *5 Rules for White Belts*, author Chris Matakas states, "Mastery is not a final point at which to arrive; it is a continuum of infinite degrees upon which we move." The Three Pillars remain receptive to new learning. If they never would have put this humility into practice, they may have never delved into the Chinese art of Hsing-I Luihebafa to supplement their training. Furthermore, all three have become students of the author in the art of SMP[1] Arnis as they feel this martial art blends extremely well into their Chi-Ryu Jiujitsu methods.

Matakas puts the concept of seeking improvement outside of your comfort zone in a very prophetic statement in his book *On Jiu Jitsu* where he writes, "It took becoming a black belt in Jiu Jitsu to realize that I am a white belt in everything else." He refers this to personal life and seeking to be better in all facets of life. However, one can very easily adjust Matakas' statement and say once you attain black belt in one system it makes you realize you are a white belt in all other systems. All serious martial artists know and understand this and take it to heart by exploring other styles and systems to not only gain new knowledge but also to enhance their understanding of their main system. Having the *shoshin* frame of mind noted earlier is essential to take your skills beyond what you think you can achieve. Grandmaster Latimer, Master Costanzo, and Master McDonald each put a large emphasis on life-long learning.

---

[1] Sining Marsiyal ng Pilipinas, or martial art of the Philippines.

Grandmaster Isham Latimer

Grandmaster Latimer has had a rich and extensive background in a variety of martial disciplines throughout his career as both a student and teacher. His training includes Isshinryu Karate, Sanuces Ryu Jujutsu, Seiryoku Jujutsu, Modern Arnis, Kobujitsu, and Hsing-I Liuhebafa Chuan.

He began his martial arts training in 1972 just after earning his BA degree in liberal arts from State University of New York at Stoney Brook under the guidance of Robert Salay and Joe Drual, both men ranked 6th Dan in Isshinryu Karate. The training also included Seiryoku Jujutsu under Sensei Drual where Grandmaster Latimer eventually earned the rank of brown belt San-kyu. After several years of training five nights per week, Grandmaster Latimer earned his shodan, 1st degree black belt, ranking in Isshinryu Karate in 1975. Soon after, he was directed to begin teaching classes both at Salay's dojo and at the local YMCA center in Huntington Village, Long Island.

After a short bit of time though, things started to get tense. As Grandmaster Latimer explains in his biography in the book *The Modern Day Warriors – In Their Own Words*, "Sensei Salay informed me that he had received a number of complaints from students that I was too tough on them. Everything that I ever asked any student to do, I worked right along with them, every repetition of every technique. I was asked to ease up the workouts a bit by Sensei Salay." After reflecting on this request and realizing it was Salay's dojo and his livelihood, Grandmaster Latimer concluded it was time to move on and concentrate on improving his own martial arts skills and knowledge.

Example of Grandmaster Latimer's painting

Grandmaster Latimer moved around working with various dojo and instructors in an effort to hone his overall skill set and understanding of fighting principles, all the while knowing in the back of his mind he wanted to find another excellent Isshinryu dojo. For a time, he worked with a Crane Kung Fu instructor at Adelphi University in Garden City, NY. Later in 1975 he became friends with Makakuvu Ali El Bey, a black belt instructor in Sanuces Ryu Jujutsu under the renowned founder of that system, Grandmaster Moses Powell. All of this experience into various other systems would begin to shape his vision of martial arts and would eventually lead to exploring combinations and fighting tactics that would ultimately lead to the process of forming Chi-Ryu Jiujitsu.

His friendship with Makakuvu led both men to work together for the betterment of the local community. Along with training together and exchanging techniques and combat applications, both men discussed many issues that affect the black community and, by extension, black martial artists. They worked together on those issues by organizing various activities such as jazz concerts, youth rallies, basketball tournaments as well as martial arts demonstrations. This is what martial arts training and involvement can foster: a community-minded effect to help your fellow man in all ways. This is the state of mind alluded to by one of Shotokan karate's leading exponents, the late Master Hirokazu Kanazawa, in his autobiography *Karate, My Life*: "In the world of budo everybody is of equal standing regardless of race, creed, or religion. Good people stand shoulder to shoulder within the great family that is the dojo." A true dojo atmosphere tends to bring out the best in everyone involved.

Grandmaster Latimer wanted badly to continue with his Isshinryu training considering the style's efficiency and practicality for street defense. The author notes in *Order of Isshin-Ryu*, "He had grown to love the Isshinryu system because of its street combat orientation in terms of the application of techniques and rapid execution of combinations." In late 1975 a friend of his, Ron Taganashi of the Nisei Goju-Ryu style, had a suggestion. Master Taganashi would go on to develop the American-Te Goju-Ryu martial arts system. American-Te utilizes Goju-Ryu karate as its foundation and incorporates a wide variety of techniques from other systems. Master Taganashi informed Grandmaster Latimer to go see Sensei Malachi Lee in New York City.

Early 1970s - Ron Taganashi, kneeling in the middle. Malachi Lee, standing in center.

Grandmaster Latimer recalls of Malachi Lee in the author's book *Order of Isshin-Ryu*, "He did not like to train his students for tournament competition. His belief was that the fight on the street will never be controlled in the manner such as the structured format of a tournament." The street defense scenario is a totally different environment than a tournament setting. The differences include: No judges, no rules, no rest, potential secondary threats, uneven surfaces, hard surfaces, and possibly various objects to contend with. Sensei Lee's training was geared towards the street environment.

Grandmaster Latimer additionally remembers of Sensei Lee, "When he interviewed me for potential membership in his dojo, we discussed my current rank and my training expectations. I told him that I ranked shodan black belt in Isshinryu under Sensei Salay and Sensei Drual; however, I was perfectly willing to begin training as a white belt because in my mind it was a new beginning for me and I would accept whatever rank he determined I had earned at such time as he saw fit. I knew that he and his students had much to offer and I would grow as a person and my martial arts skills and knowledge would advance under Sensei Lee's leadership."

The Malachi Lee dojo had very talented students including Maria Melendez, Jose Diaz, John McDonald, Aston Hugh, and Arthur Samson. It was an exceptional dojo and Grandmaster Latimer found Malachi Lee to be an outstanding instructor and martial artist. Sensei Lee's untimely death in June 1976 was a devastating jolt to Grandmaster Latimer and all of his dojo brothers and sisters. Just prior to Lee's passing, Grandmaster Latimer was elevated to the rank of San-Kyu brown belt in April 1976.

Master Lee connected with Grandmaster Toby Cooling, the founder of Order of Isshin-Ryu Karate, several years preceding his death. It was this connection and Grandmaster Latimer's resulting friendship with Grandmaster Cooling for which he acknowledges and credits much of his advancement in the art of Isshinryu Karate. In February 2011, Grandmaster Latimer was promoted by Grandmaster Cooling to the rank of Ku-Dan, 9th degree black belt, during the Order of Isshin-Ryu shiai in Chesapeake, Maryland. As he progressed through black belt rankings to that of 9th Dan, Grandmaster Latimer has been acknowledged for his dedication, skills, and loyalty to the martial arts world and was ultimately inducted into the International Isshinryu Hall of Fame in 2003.

In 2020 Grandmaster Latimer was awarded the Red Dragon Tab - Certificate of Brotherhood and Sisterhood as presented by Soke Denny Shaffer, founder of Dragon Sen-I Jutsu. This system provides a mixture of Isshin-Ryu Karate, Kickboxing, Jujitsu, Kung-Fu and Boxing. Grandmaster Shaffer has a long and illustrious martial arts background. He trained with legendary martial artists such as Bruce Lee and Grandmaster Harold Long in Isshinryu Karate. Grandmaster Shaffer was inducted into the International Isshinryu Hall of Fame in 1984. Grandmaster Shaffer states, "This award is not based on politics, religion, color, rank, or gender. It is offered by vote of the [Red Dragon] black belts, by virtue of martial arts contributions and friendship to our dojo." In 2006, Grandmaster Latimer formally began spearheading the development of a new system, Chi-Ryu Jiujitsu, which actually started many years before, albeit not in a formal manner. He collaborated over the past 20 years with his students, Master John Costanzo (8th Dan) and Sensei John McDonald (7th Dan), the co-developers of the system. They were undeniably valuable contributors in the development of Chi-Ryu Jiujitsu, which is an eclectic system comprising the skills, philosophy, and principles from Order of Isshin-Ryu Karate, Seiryoku Jujutsu, Sanuces Ryu Jujutsu, Hsing-I Liuhebafa Chuan and Modern Arnis.

In 1979, Grandmaster Latimer received his master's degree in social work from the State University of New York at Stoney Brook. He then began work at the John Jay College of Criminal Justice as an academic counselor and faculty advisor. In 1992, he attended the New York State Division of Parole Academy, graduating first in the class and receiving the Leroy Drake Award for Excellence. He worked for the Specialized Absconder Search Unit executing warrants. During his career with the New York State Division of Parole, he worked for three years as a case load worker monitoring, on average, 150 parolees each year.

In his last 11 years in the New York State Division of Parole, he was a full-time law enforcement trainer in the Staff Development Unit and an instructor on the Tactical Training Team for the following areas: firearms, defensive tactics, use of force, baton, and infectious diseases. Grandmaster Latimer retired from that unit and the Division of Parole after 23 years of service with the law enforcement community on October 31, 2012. Since 2012, he serves as President of his own business: Golden Glow Investigative & Protective Services, LLC. He holds numerous certifications with the New York State Department of Homeland Security and the New York State Division of Parole as an instructor for defensive tactics, firearms, and baton. He has received numerous commendations for high professional standards of conduct, sound tactical judgment, and restraint under critical circumstances.
Grandmaster Latimer attributes his career achievements much in part to his martial arts training, to his family, and also to the accomplishments and standards set by the masters and

practitioners of the arts who have preceded him as well as his contemporaries. He continues to strive for martial arts knowledge, human growth and development, and the most important purpose to him, which is his devotion to his family.

Master John Costanzo

Master Costanzo began his martial arts training as a student of Grandmaster Isham Latimer in 1979 and continues to train and study with him to this day. Master Costanzo's interest in the martial arts originally started in high school where he was a gymnast who was fascinated by the athleticism, inner strength and grace of the martial arts. After graduating high school, he served in the United States Army during the Vietnam War from 1968 – 1970 where he achieved the rank of Sergeant E5 as a combat infantry squad leader for the 1st Infantry Division. He was awarded the Bronze Star and the Army Commendation Medal for valor while serving his country.

Returning to civilian life, John graduated from Dowling College in 1976 with a BA majoring in Art Education under the GI Bill. He subsequently worked as a freelance illustrator creating storyboards and comps for various commercial firms in Manhattan, New York City. Several years later, he began his career with AT&T in New York and New Jersey, which lasted for 24 years. While at AT&T, he was then promoted through the ranks to a senior management programmer in charge of designing information based intranet web pages and original programs for the CEO in AT&T's WorkNet

John Costanzo with 1st Infantry Division in Vietnam.

division. Lastly, he taught Computer Science AP Java classes for 13 years at St. Joseph's High School in Metuchen, New Jersey where he eventually retired in 2016.

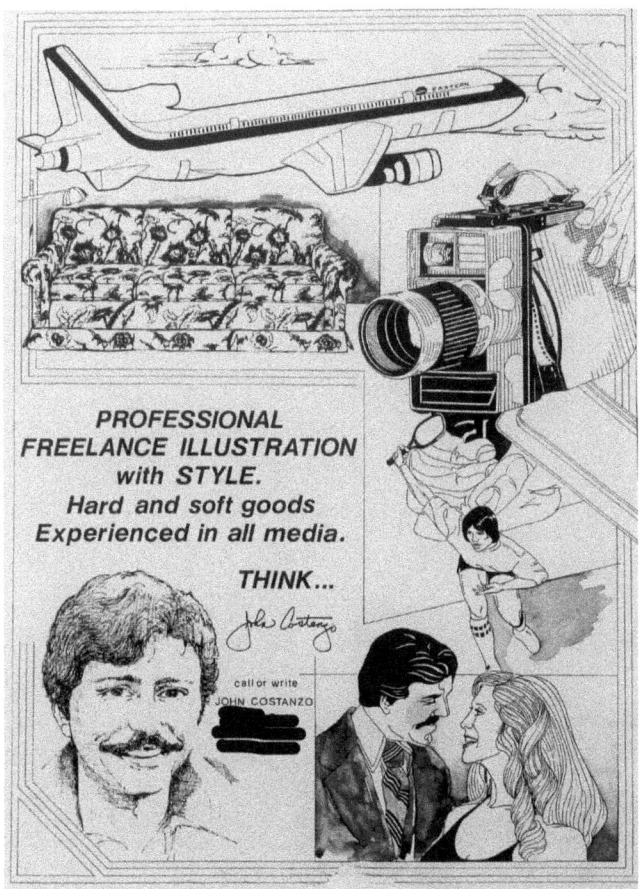

Example of Master Costanzo's graphic design work

While Master Costanzo studied under Grandmaster Isham Latimer, he simultaneously became a member of the Order of Isshin-Ryu under the direction and counsel of Grandmaster Toby Cooling. He currently holds the rank of Hachi-Dan, 8th degree black belt, in Order of Isshin-Ryu Karate.

Master Costanzo is proficient in Isshinryu hand and weapons kata in addition to his expertise in Jujitsu and self-defense techniques including knife and firearms. He has also honed his skills through deep breathing exercises, applying them within his practice of the ancient Chinese martial arts form known as Hsing-I Liuhebafa Chuan.

From this background, Master Costanzo collaborated with Grandmaster Latimer and Master John McDonald in creating the Chi-Ryu Jiujitsu system which melds techniques and concepts from Order of Isshin-Ryu Karate, Jujitsu, Liuhebafa Chuan, and self-defense techniques developed in Grandmaster Latimer's dojo.

Master Costanzo has been a martial arts instructor under the banner of the Order of Isshin-Ryu for over 35 years, teaching in Long Island, New York and currently has a non-profit dojo at the Woodbridge Community Center in New Jersey. He has a son, Matthew and a daughter, Dawn, five grandchildren and resides in Union, New Jersey with his loving partner Judith Camlin.

Master John McDonald

Master McDonald began his martial arts training in 1972 under Sensei Malachi Lee in New York City. Shortly thereafter, Sensei Lee introduced his students to Grandmaster Toby Cooling and the dojo would become a formal member of the Order of Isshin-Ryu family. Following Sensei Lee's death, Master McDonald along with Grandmaster Latimer, Jose Diaz and Maria Melendez continued running Sensei Lee's dojo under the leadership of Maria Melendez who was elevated to *sensei* status by Grandmaster Cooling. Master McDonald was elevated to the rank of sho-dan, 1st degree black belt, in 1977 by Sensei Melendez in Order of Isshin-Ryu Karate. In 2015, he was elevated to the rank of nana-dan, or 7th degree black belt.

Master McDonald continues training under Grandmaster Isham Latimer to this day. Along with his sensei and Master John Costanzo, he co-developed a new style of martial arts, Chi-Ryu Jiujitsu, by bringing to the table his skills in Isshinryu Karate, Modern Arnis, Chin Na, Liuhebafa, knife fighting and firearms.

He has a long background in the acting and stage communities. He is a 1968 graduate of Carnegie Mellon University's School of Drama in Pittsburgh, Pennsylvania. Upon graduating from Carnegie Mellon, he became the first African American to receive a BFA degree in Acting from that institution. Going by the professional name of John Danelle, his first professional acting job was as a member of the Lincoln Center Repertory Company. His Broadway credits include Alton Scales in Lorraine Hansberry's *The Sign In Sidney Brustein's Window*, directed by Alan Schneider and the dual role of Leroy Jackson (John Amos' son) and Young Luther (John Amos as a young man) in *Tough to Get Help*, directed by Carl Reiner. Off Broadway, he co-produced and originated the role of Val Johnson in Dennis McIntyre's play, *Split Second*. The critically acclaimed play is included in the *Burns and Mantle THEATRE YEARBOOK: THE BEST PLAYS OF 1984-1985*. Subsequent productions have been mounted in Los Angeles, Chicago, Detroit, Atlanta, Miami, San Diego and London. The play continues to be performed on various levels across the country. Master McDonald is known to many for his portrayal of Dr. Frank Grant on ABC-TV'S *All My Children* and Lt. Art Hindman in *Loving*. When he signed his first contract with ABC in 1972, he became only the third African American ever to be put under contract in a daytime drama.

NY Times Review for Split Second

THE NEW YORK TIMES, FRIDAY, AUGUST 10, 1984

Broadway
Enid Nemy

Lyceum next stop for comic flights of Whoopi Goldberg.

WHOOPI GOLDBERG is coming to Broadway. The 34-year-old performer, whose blend of standup comedy, political satire and straight theater has been seen primarily in fringe clubs and theaters, is being brought to the Lyceum Theater by Mike Nichols, Emanuel Azenberg and the Shubert Organization. Rehearsals for the new two-hour show, "Whoopi Goldberg Variations," will start next month, and performances will begin Oct. 6.

Miss Goldberg, described by Mr. Nichols as "one part Elaine May, one part Groucho, one part Ruth Draper, one part Richard Pryor and five parts never before seen," said the whole thing was like a dream.

"Honey, I've been walking around for days with nothing but teeth showing," Miss Goldberg said by telephone from her vacation retreat in Vermont.

As to working with Mr. Nichols, Miss Goldberg sounded ecstatic. "The man is like Moses," she said.

• • • •

Arthur Cantor, whose production credits include "On Golden Pond" and "Acting Shakespeare," has just returned from London with rights to "Pack of Lies," the suspense play by Hugh Whitemore that's been running in the West End for almost a year. The Broadway opening is planned for late January, after a run at the Eisenhower Theater in Washington. Rosemary Harris, who has won both Tony and Emmy awards, has agreed to play the role originated by Judi Dench in London, and Clifford Williams, who directed "Sleuth," will do the same for this story of a suburban couple who find that their neighbors and best friends are suspected of espionage. The play is based on a true case in England in the 1960's. Mr. Cantor's co-producer will be Bonnie

John Danelle in "Split Second": *"I'm not saying you don't work hard acting, but you work a couple of hours, and the pay is relatively good."*

John Danelle believes that acting is both an enjoyable and an easy way to make a living. As he gets to the last part of his remark, he grins ruefully and looks from side to side.

"I'm afraid actors will come out of the wall and club me," he said. "I'm not saying you don't work hard acting, but you work a couple of hours, and the pay is relatively good."

Mr. Danelle, who stars in "Split Second," a play about a black policeman who deliberately shoots a white thief who has showered him with racial insults, is serious about wanting to be known simply as an actor, rather than as a black actor. And because, for 10 years, he played Dr. Frank Grant in "All My Children" and Lieutenant Hindman on "Loving," he has also been pigeon-holed in a second category—that of soap-opera actor.

Mr. Danelle recalled that his soap opera identification was the first thing noted by Sidney Poitier when Mr. Poitier made a backstage visit after having seen "Split Second."

"He said, 'So you're a soap-opera actor,' and I said, 'No sir, I'm just an actor,'" Mr. Danelle reported. "He looked at me and said, 'That you are.' I just about died. Later on, I told him that he was one of the people responsible for my being an actor, and he said, 'In some small way, I've done the world a favor.' Can you believe it! I could have retired after that."

Mr. Danelle says that he's "not the greatest actor in the world—I just think I'm a good actor, a good craftsman." He's equally realistic about his profession.

"My primary job is to entertain," he said. "I just can't put acting on the same scale as being a doctor. I think it's important, but I can flub a line and no one dies."

In the late 1980s, John left acting to go into theatrical production. After several years as a freelance production manager, he became the first African American to be named Director of Alice Tully Hall at Lincoln Center for the Performing Arts in New York City. He went on to become first African American to be named Director of Operations at Carnegie Hall in New York City.

Master McDonald developed the concept and co-wrote the 1993 feature film *By The Sword* which stars Academy Award Winner F. Murray Abraham, Eric Roberts and Mia Sara. As a producer of the film he was a founding member of the company that arranged for the 6.5 million dollar financing as well as domestic and foreign distribution. The film was critically acclaimed by *Variety, The Hollywood Reporter, Entre Acte* and the *Los Angeles Times* and has developed a cult following among the fencing community, as well as martial artists.

1977-Sho-dan (1st degree black belt) promotion. L-R: John McDonald, Maria Melendez, Toby Cooling

He is now a private acting coach who specializes in preparing high school students who wish to become professional actors for the grueling college audition process. He has a 99.5 percent success rate and his students have been accepted at such prestigious schools as Carnegie Mellon University, Baldwin-Wallace, Cornich College of the Arts, Elon University, Emerson, Fordham, Ithaca, University of the Arts in Philadelphia, University of Hartford/The Hartt School, University of Michigan, Muhlenberg, Northwestern University, Marymount-Manhattan, NYU, Syracuse and Yale.

Master McDonald has been married for over 35 years to Cagle McDonald and has two daughters, Amanda and Mary.

SYSTEMS FORMING CHI-RYU JIUJITSU

CHAPTER 2

"When one thing moves, everything moves."
- Grandmaster Isham Latimer

The kanji for Chi-Ryu Jiujitsu is 氣流柔術. The translation in English means "the way of energy through gentle technique." Don't allow the translation to fool you. There is nothing gentle regarding the effect upon the aggressor when a Chi-Ryu Jiujitsu technique is applied in a self-defense situation. Many techniques incorporate various pressure points and joint manipulation of the body with the results being extremely painful to the attacker. Coupled with these techniques is the development of proper coordination of flowing, relaxed movement and internal energy development. When effectively combining those attributes, the attacker will generally end up causing much more harm to himself when trying to use as much power as possible in bringing aggression against the Chi-Ryu Jiujitsu practitioner.

2014 - Dobbs Ferry, New York. L - R: John McDonald, Isham Latimer, John Costanzo. The author presented his original Shodo artwork which reads "Chi-Ryu Jiujitsu."

Chi (氣), or *Ki* in Japanese, is the internal energy force one can develop through proper breathing and mental focus. *Ryu* (流), the second character, means "tradition", "school" or "way." *Jiujitsu* (柔術) is also correctly called Jujutsu. Ju can be translated to mean "gentle, soft, supple, flexible, pliable, or yielding" while Jutsu can be translated to mean "art" or "technique" and represents manipulating the opponent's force against themselves rather than confronting it with one's own force[1].

Chi-Ryu Jiujitsu is the inspiration of Grandmaster Isham Latimer, and the result of over two decades of development with his students, Master John Costanzo and Master John McDonald.

---

1 https://en.wikipedia.org/wiki/Jujutsu

In 2006, Grandmaster Latimer began to formally piece together the requirements of this new system of martial arts. With their combined experience of over 120 years in the martial arts and utilizing the creativity that each had developed from their training in both the fine and performing arts, they ultimately determined that the genesis of any skill or technique is movement. The most efficient and effective way to move is through the coordination of mind, body, and breath.

The Three Pillars together developed this eclectic style comprising the skills, philosophy, and principles from various elements from the following martial disciplines: Order of Isshin-Ryu Karate, Seiryoku Jujutsu, Sanuces-Ryu Jujutsu, Modern Arnis and Hsing-I Liuhebafa Chuan. The basis or baseline for the Chi-Ryu student regarding stances, punching, kicking, striking and the like is Order of Isshin-Ryu Karate. This provides the student with a sound foundation and a tried and true, effective system for street defense.

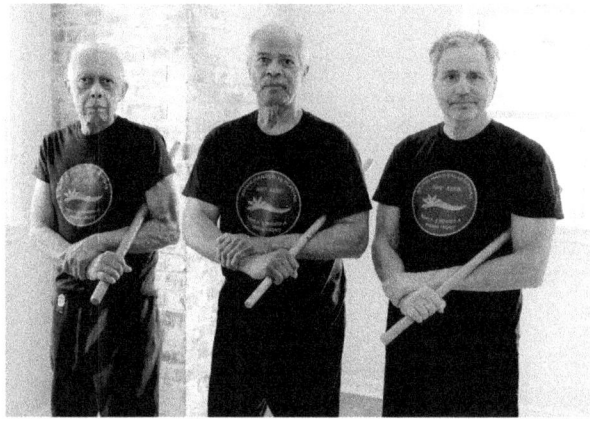

Chi-Ryu Jiujitsu incorporates Filipino martial arts into the training program. The Three Pillars formally train under the author in SMP Arnis. This art blends extremely well into the foundations and techniques of Chi-Ryu Jiujitsu.

Ultimately, as Grandmaster Latimer expresses, "A skill or technique is simply physical movement." The technique is influenced by the formal study of a particular system over time. Regardless of the style that one practices; however, every skill or technique has one fundamental element at the genesis and that is *movement,* or more specifically, *unbroken motion.* Therefore, the most efficient method of movement is essential to the effectiveness of any skill or technique. The most efficient and effective manner of movement is as natural as possible which has to do with the level of coordination between mind, body, and breath, as the movements are performed. There is a deceptive level of force in anyone's skills when these three elements are present and in harmony. This seems to be perceived by many as being something automatic. However, it is perhaps this aspect of coordination that is most difficult to learn and harness because to accomplish it one must move slowly, without ego, without intent, without stopping and starting, or with thoughts of winning and losing.

Therefore, Grandmaster Latimer has incorporated training in Hsing-I Liuhebafa Chuan, as the basis for all other skill set development in Chi-Ryu Jiujitsu. He and his collaborating black belts refer to the set movements as "forms" rather than "kata," because the term form denotes greater possibilities within movement (limitless), rather than techniques that have clearly defined parameters, including stopping and starting points. Form is intended to devoid the body and mind of being tense (muscle constrictions), during all movement. This allows for the improved chi, or qi (energy), circulation essential to achieving a higher level of oxygen throughout the circulatory system. It is also a method for achieving better overall health. Being a personal witness to the training of all three men, with a large focus on proper breathing, I can attest to the improved health benefits as all three continue to train hard into their late 70s.

Most importantly, the development of Chi-Ryu Jiujitsu began and continues to evolve in response to the infinite manner in which physical skills may be influenced by challenges to the human physique (e.g. maintaining good health and doable at any age); judicial restrictions regarding the use of force; societal attitudes towards use of force and the practitioner's purpose for training.

In 2007, I started training with Master Latimer in this martial art. I thought the Tai Chi style of movements from Liuhebafa and the breathing exercises would blend quite well with my background in Isshinryu, Arnis, and Kendo. I soon found out how deceptively complex the system is. The simple warm-up breathing exercises were extremely uncomfortable at first. I was constantly being told, "Relax. Don't tense your fingers. Let them relax and allow the energy to flow. Keep the knees slightly bent." All of this made sense and sounded easy enough, but at the end of 15 minutes of breathing exercises, my legs would shake and my feet hurt. I was used to moving around so standing still, relaxing, breathing and moving slowly and deliberately was something that took time and conscious effort before it became more natural.

Order of Isshin-Ryu Karate

Origin: Okinawa

Isshinryu karate is one of the world's most popular martial arts and is studied and practiced all across the globe. Isshinryu was officially founded on January 15, 1956 by Soke Tatsuo Shimabuku[2] (1908 – 1975), on the island of Okinawa, Japan. Isshinryu's founder studied and mastered both the Shorin-Ryu and Goju-Ryu Karate systems. These systems stem from older Okinawan fighting arts referred to as *Te* (pronounced 'tay'), meaning "hand." His Isshinryu system is a mixture of what he deemed the best aspects of both of these systems.

---

2 The more formal surname or family name is Shimabukuro.

Master Shimabuku was a highly sought after instructor on Okinawa by men serving in the United States military in the 1950s. Grandmaster Harold Long notes in his book *Isshin-Ryu Karate – The Ultimate Fighting Art*, "By 1940, he was recognized throughout the Ryukyu Islands as the foremost proponent of Shorin-ryu and Goju-ryu karate. He was the first person ever to master both systems." He also trained with Choki Motobu, who was one of the greatest fighters in the history of Okinawa. He took up the study of Okinawan weaponry such as the bo and sai from notable masters Taira Shinken and Yabiku Moden.

Grandmaster Toby Cooling earned his black belt in Isshinryu Karate under Grandmaster Tom Lewis in 1967. He also trained frequently in the dojo of Grandmaster Don Nagle in Jersey City, New Jersey. In the author's book *Order of Isshin-Ryu: One Family, One Dojo*, Grandmaster Cooling remembers, "When I heard that Master Shimabuku was still alive, I had to make a trip to Okinawa to train with him." Adding, "The way I see it, if your training means anything, you go to the source. If Grandmaster Shimabuku lived in Florida, I would've traveled there. But he happened to live in Okinawa. It didn't matter. I had to train *with* him wherever he was."

He trained with the founder of Isshinryu intensively every day since he was there as a civilian and did not hold a job. His sole purpose to be there was to train and learn from Soke Shimabuku. Grandmaster Cooling came back to the United States being elevated to roku-dan, 6th degree black belt, by Grandmaster Shimabuku and shortly after was the first to bring Isshinryu Karate to the upper eastern shore of Maryland. The 50th anniversary of Order of Isshin-Ryu Karate took place in January 2021. The Order of Isshin-Ryu family has produced many excellent martial artists over that span of time in many states and several countries.

Isshinryu Karate is known for is direct approach to self-defense. Stances tend to be mostly with the feet below the shoulders for good mobility. Straight punches and low kicks below the waist are favored for speedy execution of movements to which the opponent has a difficult time to defend. Elbow and knee strikes are added to the array of strikes to make the practitioner even more effective with a finishing type of strike. One of the main tenets of Isshinryu is that one solid punch, kick or strike should do the job and make the encounter as minimal as possible. This style prefers direct moves and strikes with the vertical fist punch, a concept introduced by Grandmaster Shimabuku that proved to be revolutionary on Okinawa in the mid-1950s. Due to the effectiveness of the first-generation students of Isshinryu Karate, the style has spread considerably throughout the world.

Another facet of Order of Isshin-Ryu Karate that plays an integral part of Chi-Ryu Jiujitsu are joint locking and joint manipulation techniques. These movements were incorporated into Order of Isshin-Ryu Karate by Grandmaster Cooling and his experiences with Chin Na, meaning 'seizing hands.' The techniques of Chin Na are highly effective in controlling your opponent or attacker by immobilizing the limbs through pressure against various points on the body. Author Yang Jwing-Ming points out in his book *Shaolin Chin Na*, "Chin Na means 'seize and control,' and mainly relies on grasping, pressing, and unnaturally twisting the sensitive parts of an opponent's body such as nerves, muscles, and joints." Yang goes on to note, "Chin Na techniques are basically independent of any martial style and can be learned by anyone willing to devote time and energy." As such, Chi-Ryu Jiujitsu includes the usage of Chin Na techniques in tandem with the other systems helping to round out the system.

Seiryoku Jujutsu

Origin: Japan

Jujutsu is one of the oldest forms of Asian fighting arts. Research shows that around the year 1600 there were over 2,000 Ko-ryu, or 'old traditions' of jujutsu. The term Jujutsu was not in use until the 17th century, after which time it became a blanket term for a wide variety of grappling-related disciplines and techniques. Jujutsu practice includes hitting or striking, punching, kicking, throwing, pinning or immobilizing, strangling, and joint locking.

The samurai of ancient Japan included jujutsu techniques in their military training which included parrying or blocking strikes, thrusts and kicks, and receiving throws or joint locking techniques while learning such skills as falling safely and knowing how to "blend" to neutralize a technique's effect. This blending in order to counter the opponent is similar to Chi-Ryu Jiujitsu's preparatory exercise called *MiXXiNG*, which will be presented in chapter five. Jujutsu practitioners also learn techniques such as releasing oneself from an enemy's grasp, and changing or shifting one's position to evade or neutralize an attack. In Chinese and Okinawan systems where the emphasis tends to be on striking, Japanese jujutsu forms differ in that there is a major emphasis upon throwing, joint lock throws, immobilizing, choke outs, and ground fighting.

Jujutsu was an integral part of the development of the well-known system of Judo, as founded by Jigoro Kano (1860 – 1938). Judo techniques generally begin with gripping the opponent, followed by off-balancing them and using their momentum against them, and then applying the technique. This is referred to as kuzushi, or the art of breaking balance[3].

---

3 https://en.wikipedia.org/wiki/Jujutsu

This concept of breaking the opponent's balance is found in many martial arts including Chi-Ryu Jiujitsu.

At the core of Kano's vision for Judo is the principle of *seiryoku zenyo*, or maximum efficient use of energy. He illustrated the application of this principle with the concept of *ju yoku go o seisu* (softness controls hardness). In short, resisting a more powerful opponent will result in your defeat, while adjusting to and evading your opponent's attack will cause him to lose his balance, his power will be reduced, and you will defeat him. This can apply to whatever the relative values of power, thus making it possible for weaker opponents to beat significantly stronger ones. This is the theory of *ju yoku go o seisu*[4].

The principle of seiryoku zenyo can apply to all types of pursuits whereby you try to fully incorporate your spiritual and physical energy to a specific purpose for the good of everyone. The Kodokan Judo Institute points out, "If directed at improving the body, it becomes a form of physical education; if applied to gaining knowledge, it will become a method of self-improvement; and, if applied to many things in society such as the necessities of life, social interaction, one's duties, and administration, it becomes a way of life[5]."

Sanuces-Ryu Jujutsu

Origin: United States

Sanuces-Ryu is an American style of jujutsu founded in 1959 by Grandmaster Moses Powell (1941 – 2005) in Brooklyn, New York. Sanuces means "survival by simplicity" and includes techniques and movements from Karate, Boxing, Arnis stick fighting and nerve and joint locks from Jujutsu. Grandmaster Powell had extensive training in martial arts systems such as

---

4 https://en.wikipedia.org/wiki/Judo
5 http://kodokanjudoinstitute.org/en/doctrine/word/seiryoku-zenyo/

Aikijujutsu, Kyusho-jutsu, Arnis and trained under Professor Florendo Visitacion, the founder of Vee-Jitsu[6].

Modern Arnis
Origin: Philippines

Historical records dating back to the 8th century show Kali (kah-lee) as the martial art of the Philippines. Late in the 16th century, the Spanish began a 400-year occupation of the islands and promptly banned the practice of Kali; however, elements of the art were hidden in plain view in the form of native dance and folk plays known as *moro-moro*. Over time, the arts resurfaced and under Spanish rule, the arts became known as eskrima, estocada, arnis de mano or arnis. Historians indicate there are as many as 200 systems of arnis, eskrima, and kali. Some of more popular styles being Illustrisimo Kali, Doce Pares Eskrima, Balintawak, Cabales Serrada, Modern Arnis, and Kombatan[7].

Filipino martial arts are now extremely popular due to the effectiveness of the techniques and the training of the weapons involved, including sticks and knives. In contrast to traditional karate systems where the student first learns empty-handed techniques, the student of Filipino martial arts begins training with weapons in hand and then progresses to empty-handed techniques at the more advanced stages. Some of the methods of training deployed within Arnis include:

Espada y daga (sword and dagger) – employs a long blade and a short dagger.
Solo baston (single stick)
Sinawali (to weave) – employs two sticks of equal length, twirled in a "weaving" fashion for blocking and striking.

Grandmaster Remy Presas (1936 - 2001) - Founder of Modern Arnis.

Chi-Ryu Jiujitsu incorporates the art of Modern Arnis within its curriculum and training. The Presas family was one of the main proponents of the martial arts of the Philippines in the United States. Grandmaster Remy Presas is the founder of Modern Arnis.

In 1977, Grandmaster Presas was in New York providing seminars on Modern Arnis. The New York dojo, located at East 23rd Street in Manhattan at this time, invited Presas to teach a week-long course for their dojo. Grandmaster Isham Latimer and Master John McDonald

---

6 https://www.tetsunami.com/tetsunami-jujutsu/sanuces-ryu/
7 http://www.presas.org/kombatan/arnishistory.htm

worked with Grandmaster Presas for eight hours each day during the week. As a result, they both earned teaching credentials in Modern Arnis at that time.

It is interesting to note that the Filipino martial arts blend extremely well with other arts including many forms of karate. In his book *Modern Arnis*, Grandmaster Presas indicates this fusion of technique by stating, "Arnis makes many martial artists discover new things about their own style. They recognize the beauty of Arnis because it blends naturally the best movements from many arts. Most of my students continue to study their own styles – they just use Arnis to supplement their understanding." Master John McDonald discovered this "blending" experience first-hand. During that week-long course at the New York dojo in 1977, they took the concept of "flow" being taught by Grandmaster Presas and, on their own, combined the movements of Modern Arnis with the kata of Isshinryu Karate. At the end of the week, they demonstrated what they came up with to Grandmaster Presas. Master McDonald recalls, "He loved it! His thing was, once you have the flow of Arnis don't keep it separate. Bring it into what you do and make it a part of your movement." Soon after working with Grandmaster Presas, the New York dojo introduced Modern Arnis to the Order of Isshin-Ryu.

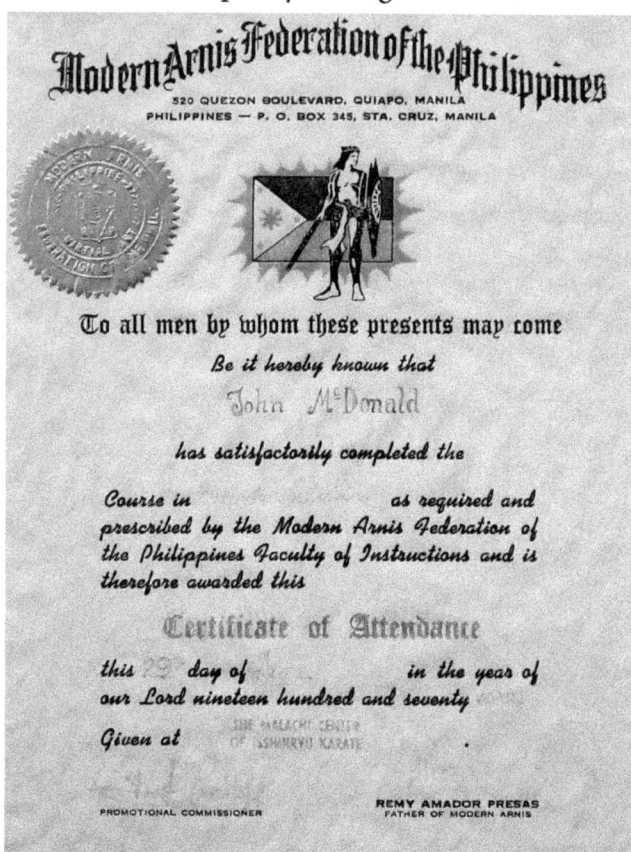

Grandmaster Latimer would eventually coordinate his Modern Arnis experiences and apply them to developing police instructor training courses during his time as a New York state parole officer. One such example, from May 1999, was for the Dutchess County Sheriff's Office in Poughkeepsie, New York. His students and co-developers of Chi-Ryu Jiujitsu assisted and supported him in this cause. Below is the syllabus and hand-written notes for the course titled *Modern Arnis – Philippine Stick Fighting*. This particular class would be the catalyst for Grandmaster Latimer to have access to all of the areas of police training and certification opportunities.

LESSON PLAN

LESSON TITLE:	COURSE:		
MODERN ARNIS - PHILLIPINE STICK FIGHTING	INSTRUCTOR DEVELOPMENT COURSE		
DURATION:	TRAINEE LEVEL:	PREPARED BY:	PAGE
50 MINUTES	INSTRUCTOR	ISHAM A. LATIMER	1 OF 3
		DATE: 5/10/99	
METHOD OF PRESENTATION:	INSTRUCTOR: ISHAM A. LATIMER		
LECTURE / DEMONSTRATION	APPROVED BY:		

INSTRUCTIONAL OBJECTIVE(S):

At the completion of this training, the trainees through observation of demonstrations the instructor provides, will be able to:

1. Identify either orally or in writing, and without reference to notes, six (6) from a total of twelve (12) striking points (targets) on the body according to the Arnis Chart on the 12 STRIKING POINTS on the body.

2. Identify either orally or in writing and without reference to notes, three (3) target areas on the body that are lethal areas according to the Monadnock Expandable Baton Chart.

3. Identify either orally or in writing and without reference to notes, one (1) out of three (3) formal exercises with the batons designed to develop coordination, timing, agility, speed and discerning vision in accordance with the information provided during this instruction.

TRAINING REFERENCES:	TRAINING AIDS REQUIRED:
Handouts	Overhead Projector
INSTRUCTOR REFERENCES:	Chalkboard
"Modern Arnis - Philippine Stick Fighting" - R.Presas	Arnis Ratan Batons
"Black Belt Magazine" - June 1981	Two (2) Assistants
Monadnock Expandable Baton Chart	

Lesson Plan

Lesson Title
Modern Arnis "Philippine Stick Fighting"

I. Introduction: 5 min.
II. Objectives
III. Presentation: 30 min.

A. Proper Grip:
B. Stances:
 1. Attention Stance
 2. Open-leg Stance
 3. Straddle-leg Stance
 4. Forward Stance
 5. Back Stance
C. "12" Basic Strikes:
 1. Right Temple
 2. Left Temple
 3. Right Shoulder
 4. Left Shoulder
 5. Groin
 6. Right side of Chest
 7. Left side of Chest
 8. Right Knee
 9. Left Knee
 10. Right Eye
 11. Left Eye
 12. Crown of Head (Top)
D. Formal Exercises:
 1. Redunda
 2. Single Sinawali
 3. Double Sinawali
E. Defense and Counter (against a #3 strike)
 1. Weakside
 a. Finger Press
 b. Wrist lock and Counter Strikes
 c. Wrist lock, disarm, parry and Counter Strikes

The blending of Arnis with other forms of martial arts continues with the Ch-Ryu Jiujitsu curriculum. The traditional MiXXiNG drill is performed without weapons. Combining the knife drill exercises of Arnis into the practice of the MiXXiNG drill adds another layer of experience and growth. As martial artists, you need to "think outside the box" and figure out how to blend and layer various exercises and drills in order to expand your skill sets, understanding, and overall flow of movement and technique. Without it, techniques tend to remain confined to rigid patterns, which is counterintuitive to actual self-defense needs.

Hsing-I Liuhebafa Chuan

Origin: China

An extensive part of the Chi-Ryu Jiujitsu curriculum is Hsing-I Liuhebafa Chuan, also known as Six Harmonies Eight Methods Boxing[8] and Water Boxing. Six Harmonies pertain to the unification of the body, while Eight Methods refer to practical applications of the techniques. This discipline was developed in China by Chen Xi Yi, who was known as a pioneer of the internal forms of martial arts. Chen was a Taoist sage during the Song Dynasty (960-1279)[9]. The actual name of the style is "Hua Yue Xi Yi Men," whereas Liuhebafa is merely a description of the principles involved. Chen Xi Yi was known for his advanced theories on philosophical Taoism, Buddhism and Confucianism. "Xi" is what cannot be heard; "Yi" is what cannot be seen[10].

Grandmaster Latimer performing Liuhebafa form.

Liuhebafa has core principles and training methods not found in other martial arts. The most important aspect of the system is mind and intention. Intention should be sharply focused on each movement, and the movements are led by mind and intention[11]. Another of the main tenets of the system is internal strength – not from muscles, but rather from tendons and bones (i.e. the structure of the body). This internal strength is developed through its training methods such as 12 short drills, or movements, repeated continuously on both sides in the spirit of slower Tai Chi motion. There is also a form, called Zhu Ji, which consists of 66 movements. Zhu Ji contains no repeating movements and when performed correctly in the spirit of proper speed found in Tai Chi Chuan can take up to 40 minutes to perform. So generally speaking, the student of Liuhebafa Chuan initially must learn the correct postures of the system while over time slowly learn to cultivate internal energy through sound breathing and appropriate intentions of the mind and body in coordination with each other. Overall, mind, intention, spirit and chi should coordinate with the external body movements.

---

8   https://en.wikipedia.org/wiki/Liuhebafa
9   https://en.wikipedia.org/wiki/Song_dynasty
10 Liuhebafa Chuan – The 4th Internal Art, by Nomura Akihiko. Hiden Budo & Bujutsu Magazine (Japan)
11 http://www.wudanglongmen.com/liuhebafa.html

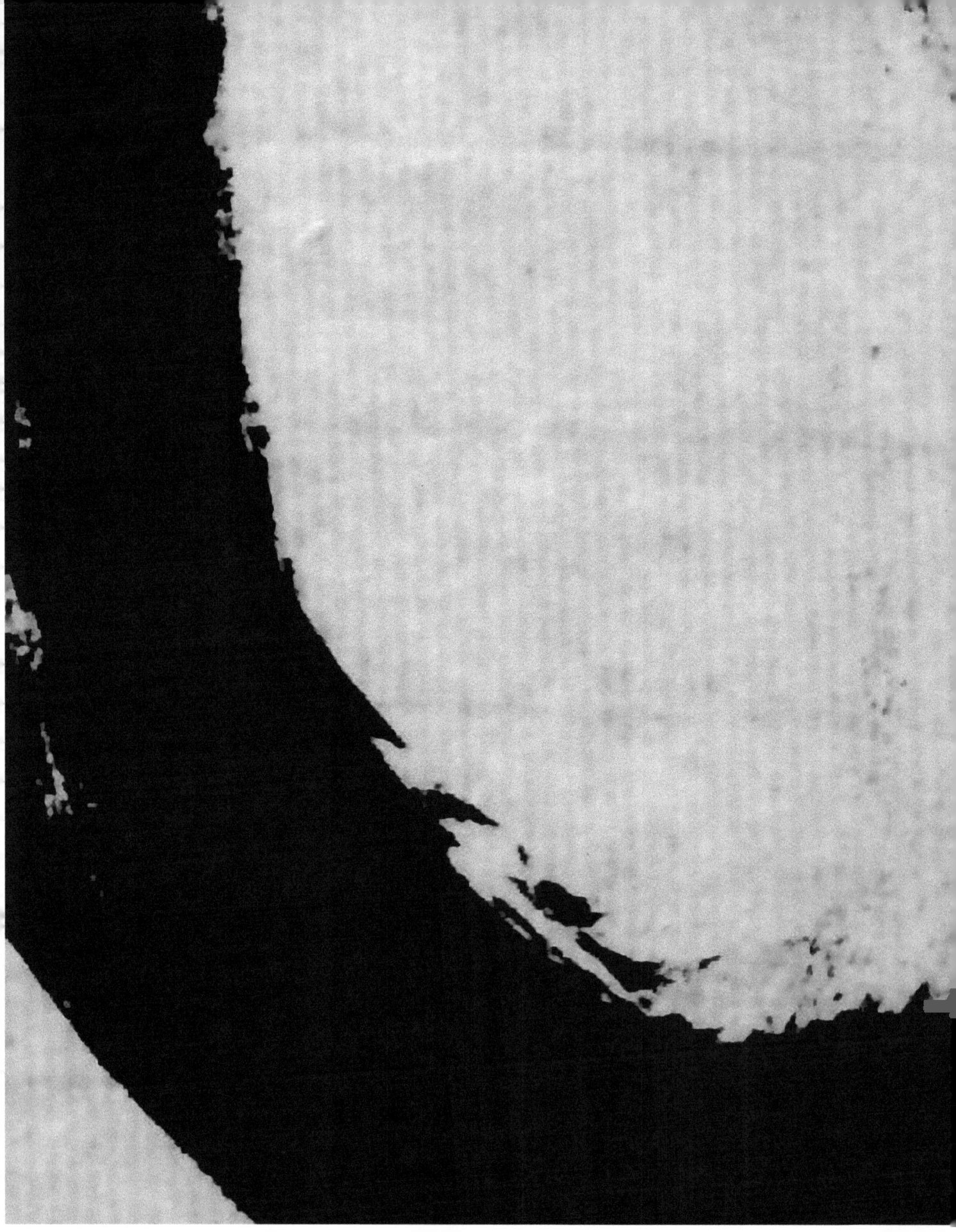

DEVELOPMENT OF CHI-RYU JIUJITSU

CHAPTER 3

"A true martial artist is not one who fears change, but one who causes it to happen."
- Grandmaster Ed Parker

The main roots of Chi-Ryu Jiujitsu come from Isshinryu Karate. As such, the various punches and kicks and the areas of the hands and feet used to deploy those strikes stem from karate. But Grandmaster Latimer had the good fortune of having exposure to a variety of different arts available in New York City and the surrounding area. As you might imagine, this part of the United States was a literal melting pot of martial arts styles and practitioners back in the 60s, 70s and 80s. He was able to collaborate with many outstanding martial artists who trained and competed with other top-notch competitors of the day. Although gaining exposure to many systems, Grandmaster Latimer still wanted to find a good Isshinryu school to continue training in that system. A friend from the Nisei Goju Ryu system, Ron Taganashi, suggested he look into Malachi Lee's Isshinryu school. The rest is history. Sensei Lee and his students so impressed him during his first visit to the dojo that he made up his mind to join that very evening. He remembers of the dojo on that initial visit, "Everyone was serious and busy, and that was even before Sensei Lee walked onto the dojo floor! I immediately knew I found the place I wanted to be."

The training at Lee's dojo was always a test of sheer willpower. Grandmaster Latimer stated in the author's book *Order of Isshin-Ryu*, "I thought to myself, 'That man has got to be crazy!' He would work you past your limits, and then bring you back. He had a lot of energy and would bring the same out in you." Grandmaster Latimer and Master McDonald trained together in the New York City dojo where they both remembered, "It was normal during many classes that students worked only three techniques. The key was that they were repeated as many as 500 times, from various stances and in various combinations." They also noted mats were made of a hard rubber material and covered with sail cloth. Sensei Lee had them specially made that way. It became an unwritten requirement for the sweat to soak through your gi and leave your silhouette on the dojo mat. And heat in the winter and air conditioning in the summer were non-existent. In the Malachi Lee dojo, you were essentially left to your own devices to maintain body temperate just to get through each workout.

Grandmaster Latimer had the privilege of being Sensei Lee's student until his untimely death in 1976. One of Lee's top students, Sensei Maria Melendez, subsequently promoted Grandmaster Latimer and Master McDonald to sho-dan, or 1st degree black belt, after formally joining the Order of Isshin-Ryu Karate family.

Martial artists are continually looking to improve their skills. They are always reviewing their processes and approach to training in a never-ending journey to move farther along the path to reach higher levels of understanding of what the martial arts has to offer. This journey should also include exposure to many other styles and systems to complement your main style of study. At a certain point in training, the individual must move from practicing a specific martial art to becoming a well-rounded martial artist. This is precisely what happened with the Three Pillars of Chi-Ryu Jiujitsu. They took the initiative upon themselves to seek out other systems and gain priceless exposure to techniques and fighting concepts. Grandmaster Toby Cooling of the Order of Isshin-Ryu makes the point in *Order of Isshin-Ryu – One Family, One Dojo*, "Without changing the move of the kata, if you have a better bunkai (interpretation), then show it to me and I'll use it. I want to continue to learn." This is what masters and grandmasters of the martial arts understand. The learning, refining, adjusting and improving never ends. The drive to continue learning is not simply a statement for the sake of humility. It's a commitment for the artist who is truly serious about their training.

The development of Chi-Ryu Jiujitsu was always an ever-present concept in the mind of Grandmaster Latimer throughout his training. He is the creative inspiration and catalyst for the Chi-Ryu Jiujitsu system. He worked intensely with his students and co-developers Master John Costanzo and Master John McDonald on formatting the system and curriculum. Master Costanzo notes, "Grandmaster Latimer has always aspired to expanding his martial arts knowledge since he started his training almost 50 years ago, long before his journey found its way to Chi-Ryu Jiujitsu. As his student for the last 40 years, I have been a witness and active participant in this evolution."

Soon after Grandmaster Latimer achieved his black belt in Isshinryu and his brown belt in Seiryoku Jujutsu under Sensei Drual and eventually joining Sensei Malachi Lee's Isshinryu dojo, fate would lead him to the Order of Isshin-Ryu.

It was Grandmaster Cooling who always encouraged his black belts to seek out knowledge and bring it back to the Order of Isshin-Ryu. Costanzo states, "Grandmaster Latimer took this directive literally and with a vengeance. During this time, I trained vigorously in all of the Order of Isshin-Ryu requirements and their strict adherence to high standards but I was also Grandmaster Latimer's main *uke*, or training partner, while he studied and created various fighting techniques over the years." In reality, from nearly the very beginning of his martial arts journey, Grandmaster Latimer could see and envision the benefits of creating his own combinations of self-defense moves. His development of these techniques and defense scenarios would literally serve as a forecast to his journey toward the creation of Chi-Ryu Jiujitsu.

According to Master Costanzo, this cycle went on for years but the hunger to expand their knowledge base was always present. He explains the cycle of exploration this way, "I personally felt that I was searching for something that would piece together a concept that had alluded me. Looking back, some words that come to mind to describe that 'something' was encompassing fluidity, calmness of mind and body, and a more intuitive awareness of movements around me. I was unsure what to do with these thoughts. As it turns out, sometimes you look for it and sometimes it actually finds you. It was then that Grandmaster Latimer introduced [myself and Master McDonald] to MiXXiNG, more than two decades ago. This practice drill fit perfectly into our core philosophy, which is *when one thing moves, everything moves*." Over time, MiXXiNG helps the Chi-Ryu Jiujitsu student develop an acute awareness of the opponent's movements while maintaining a calm mind, body and breath.

The next major chain in the development of Chi-Ryu Jiujitsu came from an old acquaintance of Grandmaster Latimer and Master McDonald. Master Aston Hugh was a fellow Isshinryu black belt from the New York dojo of the Order of Isshin-Ryu system. He introduced the Three Pillars to a Chinese form of martial arts that predates Tai Chi Chuan, called Hsing-I Liuhebafa Chuan. Master Hugh taught them the long form of Liuhebafa. Performed correctly, this form takes from eight to ten minutes to complete. Master Costanzo reflects the following regarding Liuhebafa training, "The slow, deliberate controlled breathing synchronized with the fluid movements of Liuhebafa has enriched me as a martial artist as well as in my private life. Merging the concepts from decades of martial arts training along with integrating MiXXiNG and Liuhebafa was the birth of Chi-Ryu Jiujitsu."

A major emphasis or mental focal point of Chi-Ryu Jiujitsu training is on continuous growth. Certainly, this is the general mindset and training pattern of the Three Pillars. Without growth in all facets of martial arts, there is an absence of meaning to the overall pursuit. Master John McDonald explains regarding the overall development of Chi-Ryu Jiujitsu techniques, "We didn't pick and choose specific techniques from various systems. We selected moves that flowed well together and then took them even further to increase their efficiency and effectiveness." Grandmaster Latimer adds, "We considered the most effective moves defensively." [The Three Pillars] then talked out all these moves over and over again to ensure the most tactically sound motion. Master McDonald further explains how the techniques are continuously scrutinized for adherence to continuous growth, "The techniques you see are where they are at that particular moment. We always try to make them better. Improvement is not a static thing."

As a martial artist, at some point in your training, you must begin to relate your training to all facts of your daily life. Observing and understanding as many concepts from other areas to apply to your training proves quite helpful. What are the thoughts and processes behind your favorite artist or athlete? What are principles followed by a respected author or chef? Whatever they may be, they surely can be applied to your martial arts. Delve into other worthy endeavors and learn from them as excellence applies across the board regardless of your particular pursuit. The famous Shotokan karate-ka Hirokazu Kanazawa explains in his book *Karate – My Life*, "Our seniors would continuously advise us that karate is not something you do just in the dojo. Everything you see or do outside is related. You should always be thinking about karate. It doesn't matter if you're watching baseball, dancing, sumo, kendo, or aikido, you should always observe them with an eye to make use of it in your karate. That's how you've got to live."

Kanazawa took this advice from his seniors well. At one point, he studied Tai Chi for a time and relates in his autobiography, *Karate – My Life*, how it helped his Shotokan performance, "Even though my study of Tai Chi was brief, it gave me a new understanding of the nunchaku, bo, and other aspects of the classical Okinawa martial arts, such as the ability to exert yourself without exerting yourself. In a similar vein, I also learned many things from Aikido. Using some of this knowledge, I developed a *mawari-oi-tsuki* (roundhouse lunge punch) to deal with the big fellows I encountered in Europe [in competition]."

Martial artists develop an awareness of not only the principles of their main system of training and study, but they tend to gravitate to various other systems of martial arts. The reasons for this would likely be as vast and complex as the personalities behind them. Generally speaking, as men and women of martial arts gain a degree of proficiency, they often look into other systems not only out of basic curiosity but to expand awareness and knowledge considering the amount of time required to develop skill in their chosen system. This awareness may come from introductory courses or seminars to demonstrations, to actually joining a dojo or school and taking up training in another system in tandem with their main style. Regardless of how and why someone wants to gain this additional exposure, for a serious martial artist it essentially becomes a necessity to fully understand their main system of training.

The founder of Judo, Jigoro Kano, made this point explicitly to his followers. It is said at one time he attended a seminar by the founder of Aikido, Morihei Ueshiba, and was so impressed that he stated Aikido was the ideal budo, the real Judo. Kano believed that you must be interested in all martial arts if you want to progress and advance your skills in your particular style. Just pick up any book on martial arts or study the biographies of any particular high ranking or well-known proponent of their art and you'll find that cross-training of various systems or styles of martial arts are at the core of the history behind those people. The examples of this multi-system approach to training and research are seemingly endless.

According to Grandmaster Latimer, his focus in recent years has been that of health-related issues among martial artists today. He feels that as martial artists, we may overlook the fact that there is more to maintaining good health than how hard we can punch, kick, perform kata, do kumite, and apply joint manipulation techniques, etc… Much of what we know and can physically perform is the result of our state of overall health including mental, physical, and emotional. We should not neglect things like good nutrition, proper rest, and positive thinking.

With the inclusion of Liuhebafa training into the Chi-Ryu Jiujitsu system, the focus of health improvement is well-established. Although not exactly the same as Tai Chi Chuan, Liuhebafa is an internal martial art similar to Tai Chi in its performance as well as health benefits. Many people all over the world take up Tai Chi practice precisely for what it has to offer for an improved quality of life. Author Da Liu expresses in his book *Tai Chi Chuan and I Ching*, "It [Tai Chi] has the advantages of regular exercise combined with a definite emphasis on the gracefulness and slowness of pace that Western society so conspicuously lacks. Tai Chi Chuan can give those who live in industrialized fast-paced cities a compensating factor in their lives. It relaxes the mind as well as the body. It helps digestion, quiets the nervous system, benefits heart and blood circulation, makes joints loose, and refreshes the skin." Every Chi-Ryu Jiujitsu training session includes both breathing exercises as well as practice of the Liuhebafa form, both of which are presented later in this book. The idea is that martial arts is a lifetime path to follow. If the body breaks down over time due to continuously tense muscle exertion, hard breathing, and joint damage, then you will be unable to participate after a point in time. Chi-Ryu Jiujitsu aims to keep the participant active and going well into advanced age and Liuhebafa is the vehicle to achieve this desired state.

The formulation of any martial art is a visionary process that cannot be understated. It's not easy to literally 'put yourself out there' and declare a new art. All systems of martial arts are the training method of the founder, developed over years and years of intense, challenging effort. All such founders systematized their techniques that they felt provided the best defensive tactics in light of their physical and mental attributes and collective training experiences. In the broadest sense, the martial arts system is meant to facilitate growth. This growth comes from new and often quite difficult experiences. Creating a martial arts system is a venture into the unknown. As Ryan Holiday writes in his book *Courage is Calling*, "All growth is a leap in the dark. If you're afraid of that, you'll never do anything worthwhile. If you take counsel in your fears, you'll never take that step, make that leap." The Three Pillars of Chi-Ryu Jiujitsu are not about to sit around doing the same thing. They're not afraid of what's not known or what isn't conventional. They continually explore and push the envelope of their training methods and tactics to pursue such growth.

BREATHING EXERCISES

"The way of internal energy is through the coordination of mind, body and breath."

- Grandmaster Isham Latimer

The proper execution of breathing could very well be the most important aspect of improvement within your martial arts training. Article Thirteen within Patrick McCarthy's book *Bubishi* is titled *The Eight Precepts of Quanfa*. Precept number three states, "Inhaling represents softness while exhaling characterizes hardness." The great Okinawan karate master Chojun Miyagi, when looking for a name for his system of martial arts selected this precept to label his karate Goju-Ryu. Goju-Ryu refers to these eight precepts as Kempo Hakku, or The Eight Poems of the Fist. When we inhale and exhale the power of *go* can be combined with the softness of *ju* for a more complete development of technique.

Breathing is so secondary in nature that we tend to forget the importance it has in maintaining sound health and control over your body and its reaction to external forces. Martial arts consist of both external techniques, physical motion and development, and internal concepts such as breathing, chi energy, and spiritual development. However, the focus on martial arts training tends to be limited to or remain only on external development and performance. It seems more and more, the internal aspects of training are given trivial amounts of time and consideration by current martial artists. Dr. Yang, Jwing-Ming makes the point in his book *Qigong*, "When the Oriental martial arts were imported to the Western world, because of traditional secrecy, the modern life-style, and the different cultural background, there was a separation between the training of the external techniques and the internal cultivation. This has made the arts and the training incomplete."

Considering the number of molecules in the air that we inhale and exhale with every breath, how we breathe is equally as important as our diet and exercise. Chi-Ryu Jiujitsu brings back the importance of proper breathing into the training curriculum. There has to be a committed effort to continually think about and focus on your breathing in order to improve. The late Hirokazu Kanazawa makes this point well in his biographical book *Karate, My Life*: "Including budo, much of traditional Japanese culture is centered around 'ma' and 'kokyu.' The former refers to the space and distance between two objects, events, or times, and the latter to the act of inhaling and exhaling. I like looking at big pieces of calligraphy. I can follow the calligrapher's brush stroke where it first makes contact with the paper until around where it fades out. From this, I can imagine how they were breathing."

Breath control is your starting point for maintaining mental toughness as well as controlling the nervous system that is so essential in controlling movement and reaction. Kanazawa makes the point strongly regarding breath control in his book where he states, "Ninety percent of people do not know how to breathe correctly. If your breathing is wrong, your body will be wrong and your mind will be wrong." As Mark Devine of SealFit points out on YouTube, "Proper breathing is where to begin in order to gain control over a situation." This may include fear, stress, anxiety, or worry. Devine continues, "Every breath pattern has a corresponding emotional pattern to it. Fear leads to shortness of breath or panting, an erratic pattern." When your mind takes over your thoughts leading to such things as fear, your breathing will suffer, making it difficult to control what is at hand. You must control your breath, which is the one thing you can rely on. Devine explains, "If you're not aware of your breath, then you're out of control. First action is to come back to the breath, and check in with it, develop an intimate awareness of it (slow it down)."

Learning to breathe correctly and control your body's movement and reactions became a large part of Rickson Gracie's training program. In his book *Breathe* he explains how improving his breathing technique took his fighting skills within the grappling arena to a much higher level as he developed into a meditative state of mind when his breathing was focused and purposeful. Gracie notes, "If you are moving and breathing, you can't have other thoughts in your head. You can't think, then move and breathe; it's not the same." When Gracie developed his breathing to such a degree, he expressed the result this way, "I was able to focus with absolute clarity and my senses grew sharper, as did my awareness of my body and surroundings."

Exercise and movement are controlled and affected by the nervous system. A sound nervous system allows the muscles to stretch and contract in concert with your breathing. All of this is influenced by the mind; however, without proper breathing the mind can override your nervous system and cause inappropriate movement or reactions. When you are calm, the body is able to remain relaxed. When you are relaxed, you can then move efficiently and effectively. Devine goes into detail as follows, "You need to interrupt the improper or unhelpful breathing pattern, and replace it with a deep breathing pattern that we associate with calmness. Then we will feel more calm and in control. This happens because the emotional energy pattern will begin to change, and you also trigger the parasympathetic nervous system that overrides the crises mode sympathetic nervous system which produces the hormones such as adrenaline and cortisol." As we can see, everything begins with proper breathing and control over your breathing patterns. And the benefits go beyond self-defense techniques.

2021 - Hastings on Hudson, NY - Master John McDonald performing controlled breathing prior to a training session.

There is considerable science behind breathing to support the benefits of proper breathing and the adverse effects of improper breathing. In the *Wall Street Journal*, James Nestor writes in a May 21, 2020 article 'The Healing Power of Proper Breathing', "While interviewing neurologists, rhinologists and pulmonolists at Standford, Harvard and other institutions, what they found is that breathing habits were directly related to physical and mental health. Breathing properly can allow us to live longer and healthier lives. Breathing poorly, by contrast, can exacerbate and sometimes cause a laundry list of chronic diseases: asthma, anxiety, attention deficit hyperactivity disorder, hypertension and more. Poor breathing habits can even change the physical structure of our skeletons, depleting essential minerals and weakening our bones."

An interesting point Nestor also provides in his article concerns a visit to your doctor when you're not feeling well. Typically, your doctor will run through the standard questions about your lifestyle such as diet, sleep patterns, stress at work or at home, and discuss the seasonal allergies to which you may be sensitive. But how often does your doctor bring up the subject of proper breathing? We all know doctors perform a check of your breathing with a stethoscope; however, this is from the perspective to see if your lungs are clear and sounding healthy, not to find out if you are breathing properly every day. Yet, how you breathe can affect or improve all of the general topics that your doctor brings up during those visits. Therefore, it becomes imperative as you grow older to keep the process of proper breathing in your conscious thoughts, so you can remain healthy.

Regarding additional science, Nestor points out, "Starting around [age] 30, bones in the chest become thinner and collapse inward. We lose about 12 percent of our lung capacity by the time we hit 50, and then the decline speeds up." *Harvard Health Publishing, as of March 2016, makes the point,* "All of us are born with the knowledge of how to fully engage the diaphragm to take deep, refreshing breaths. As we get older, however, we get out of the habit.

Everything from the stresses of everyday life to the practice of 'sucking in' the stomach for a trimmer waistline encourages us to gradually shift to shallower, less satisfying 'chest breathing.'" But with proper breathing techniques, we can actually reverse this trend.

The science behind these findings are not recent. Nestor discloses the following in his research article, "In the 1980s, researchers with the Framingham Study, a 70-year research program focused on heart disease, gathered two decades of data from 5,200 subjects, crunched the numbers and discovered that the greatest indicator of life span wasn't genetics, diet or the amount of daily exercise, as many had suspected. It was lung capacity. Larger lungs equaled longer lives. Because big lungs allow us to get more air in with fewer breaths. They save the body from a lot of unnecessary wear and tear." With information like this, it begins to make you wonder why this isn't discussed more openly in the news, at the doctor's office, in our schools, or in the case of those who study the martial arts within the karate dojo. Breathing is, of course, brought up during martial arts training, but it tends to take a back seat to topics such as fighting, bag training, weapons training, and kata or forms. Quite frankly, the research noted previously should cause all martial artists to consider reversing the order of importance in their training curriculum's.

Proper breathing helps to circulate your chi or ki energy, which originates in the lower abdomen. Da Liu explains in *Tai Chi Chuan and I Ching*, "Breathing involves the circulation of the inner vital force called *chi*. In order to accomplish deep inner breathing, one must concentrate the chi into a psychic center known as the *tan dien*, located three inches below the navel." Along with proper breathing and mental focus on your chi, the circulation of blood is improved. This is the goal of both the breathing exercises presented as well as the Liuhebafa form introduced later.

In Japanese, this is referred to as the *seika-tanden*. As Kanazawa explains, "In karate the lower body is loaded and the upper body is empty or relaxed. Interval and breathing are controlled by the lower body, which unleashes the energy to execute punches and kicks." When proper breathing is coupled with controlled, flowing movements, the effect can take on a state of meditation, but from a standing perspective. Anyone who witnesses a master of Tai Chi can attest that it appears as if they are meditating while they are moving through the sequences of the form. Ultimately, this 'state' of breathing and motion can heal injuries and past trauma and allow for better freedom of movement as well as remove stress and anxiety.

The student of Chi-Ryu Jiujitsu must learn how to control tension and relaxation of both muscle and mind. This is critical to successful application of the Chi-Ryu Jiujitsu techniques. As C.W. Nicol notes in *Moving Zen*, "The person who hardens his body, believing that physical strength will protect him, has fear within him. He has made presumptions. Moreover, that very rigidity of muscle, bone and sinew in his body can cause it to transmit the shock waves of a fast, focused blow. This is not the course an advanced karate-ka takes. He learns to be hard, and then soft. He must have dual nature of steel and water."

Kanazawa explains, "Gokui (innermost teachings) can only be learned properly through many years of austere training. They are not things that can be mastered merely through reading about them." If you take a look at anyone, in any field, who is highly skilled in their craft, it has only happened due to many years of hard work, trial and error, and someone there to provide consistent guidance. Each time I train in Chi-Ryu Jiujitsu, I always obtain correction and adjustment of a variety of techniques. I've been training in Isshinryu karate for 40 years so I have a good level of confidence in my performance of martial arts. However, I must be willing to let go of expectations, stay humble and open-minded, and accept there is still so much more to learn. Chi-Ryu Jiujitsu provides me this opportunity.

Breathing Warm-Ups

The breathing warm-up exercises of Chi-Ryu Jiujitsu are very much the cornerstone of the system. Every training session generally begins with these five movements. The breathing must be slow and deliberate on both the inhale and exhale. As James Nestor points out in his book *Breath*, "…the best way to prevent many chronic health problems, improve athletic performance, and extend longevity was to focus on how we breathed, specifically to balance oxygen and carbon dioxide levels in the body. To do this, we'd need to learn how to inhale and exhale slowly." Nestor discloses, on average, the inhale and exhale should both be approximately 5.5 seconds. The Chinese refer to this type of conscious breathing as *qigong*.

Learning to breathe properly and optimizing your breathing can improve the nervous system, boost immunity, and lower pain. Wim Hof states in his book *The Wim Hof Method*, "Alkalizing the body with the breath will start to reduce the inflammation that brings you pain." This requires consistent practice of proper breathing methods, which the Chi-Ryu Jiujitsu warm-ups can provide.

Proper breathing comes with an understanding of proper diaphragmatic breathing. According to the Cleveland Clinic website, diaphragmatic breathing is intended to help you use the diaphragm correctly while breathing in order to strengthen the diaphragm, decrease the work of breathing by slowing your breathing rate, decrease oxygen demand, and use less effort and energy to breathe.

Harvard Health Publishing, from their March 2016 article noted previously, explains as follows, "Diaphragmatic breathing (also called "abdominal breathing" or "belly breathing") encourages full oxygen exchange — that is, the beneficial trade of incoming oxygen for outgoing carbon dioxide. Not surprisingly, this type of breathing slows the heartbeat and can lower or stabilize blood pressure."

The Cleveland Clinic provides a check on proper diaphragmatic breathing technique. Start by lying on your back on a flat surface, with your knees bent and your head supported. Place one hand on your upper chest and the other just below your rib cage. This will allow you to feel your diaphragm move as you breathe. Article One in McCarthy's *Bubishi* stresses proper alignment by stating, "To encourage perfect diaphragm breathing, the spine must be parallel to the stomach." Avoid any hunched over or bent spine positioning when consciously working on checking your breathing pattern. Breathe in slowly through your nose so that your stomach moves out against your hand. The hand on your chest should remain as still as possible. Tighten your stomach muscles, letting them fall inward as you exhale through pursed lips. Again, the hand on your chest must remain as still as possible.

Chi-Ryu Jiujitsu training sessions usually begin with breathing warm up exercises. Utilizing breath, posture, and movement together in tandem helps to create a healthy body that is energetic and free from pain. Combining these three elements creates a dynamic effect of improved health, strength, and freedom of movement. "When you inhale through your nose, the sinuses release a boost of nitric oxide," as explained by James Nestor in his book *Breath*. "This molecule plays an essential role in increasing circulation and delivering oxygen to the cells." It allows our bodies to absorb considerably more oxygen than from breathing with the mouth. So, the next time you exercise or participate in some other physical activity like shoveling snow, try forcing yourself to inhale only through your nose during a break. Your recovery and getting your breathing back to normal should be a much faster.

Using our limbs, bones, and muscles to bend and stretch affects chi circulation and enables us to improve the body. Other disciplines have made this realization as well including Tai Chi and Yoga. When executed properly, Chi-Ryu Jiujitsu breathing exercises can take up to 30 minutes to perform. Although these movements are performed very slowly and deliberately, the author can attest that when finished the student will feel thoroughly warmed up and ready to begin the training session for the day.

Put your conscious thought on the execution of your breathing. Where the mind goes, the energy and the body will follow. The mind controls the whole system. When you do this you are facilitating the process of providing your entire body with appropriate energy. "The mind is a neurological muscle," explains Wim Hof in his book, "that is able to influence your body's molecular systems and aid its absorption of oxygen, which creates the energy you want." When you combine breath and movement, you should not focus on power but rather staying relaxed so circulation of blood is improved. Blood is vital and the blood is the transportation system carrying nutrients and oxygen to make the body strong. If you tense up and force the power, you will tense your muscles, especially around the chest, and your breathing will become unnatural.

Inhale gently through your nose with the tip of your tongue at the intersection of the hard palate and upper row of teeth. When you expand your stomach out, this will pull your diaphragm down and as you inhale, it will enable you to fill your lungs from the bottom up. Then slowly exhale through your nose again, but even slower than the inhale. This slow, deliberate breathing serves to boost circulation to the brain and your body. The deliberate focus on proper breathing coupled with controlled movement serves to train your connective tissue including the fascia, tendons, and ligaments of your body. Improving the condition of your connective tissue is imperative for an overall strong and healthy body. The breathing exercises serve to strengthen this connective tissue and bone rather than focusing on muscle.

Breathing Movement #1 - Gathering Breath (3 repetitions)

The first breathing movement in the Chi-Ryu Jiujitsu curriculum is called gathering breath. After each of the breathing exercises presented in this chapter, you then execute three gathering breath movements before moving to the next exercise or movement in the sequence. There is a total of five breathing movements in the Chi-Ryu Jiujitsu system.

Stand with your feet shoulder width apart; turn your toes outward slightly and bend your knees just a little. This position allows the pelvic girdle area to open in order to allow for your *chi*, or energy, to circulate through that area more effectively. Bring your arms up just outside the width of your body until the tips of your fingers on both hands nearly touch each other in the center around your forehead level. Let your hands fall slowly down the center of your body with your palms facing you until they pass your hip level. Repeat the motion two more times.

1 – Standing relaxed with feet approximately shoulder width.

2 – Simultaneously, slowly breathe in through your nose and bend your knees slightly. Your hands remain relaxed and slowly begin to raise them upward.

3 – Continue slowly breathing in and raising your hands up to the sides. Your body also rises slowly along with the rise in your hands.

4 – Complete the inhale when your open hands almost meet in front of your forehead. Fingertips should be facing each other in this position.

5 – Begin to slowly exhale while your hands lower slowly in front of you. Your also lower your center of gravity slightly during the exhale by bending the knees.

6 – Complete the repetition by lowering your hands all the way and begin the process over again for a total of three breaths.

When you perform gathering breath, there are specific mental thoughts you should entertain as if you are engaged in moving meditation.

- As you breathe in and out imagine the center of your palm as the inhale and exhale port for the energy of your body.
- On the inhale, think skeletal structure (bone). On the exhale, think soft tissue or blood.
- On the inhale, expand like a balloon or a frog would breathe. On your exhale, contract your lungs slowly to fully remove all air from the lungs.

Breathing Movement #2 – Open Right & Open Left (6 repetitions o each side)

1 - Starting with feet shoulder width apart, toes pointing slightly out, and knees slightly bent. Keeping your arms close to your body, bring both hands up to your chest area.

2 - Upon reaching your upper body, turn your palms away from your body and extend your right arm to the rear and your left arm to the front.

3 - Both hands are moving in 45-degree angles respectively in relation to your body. Your eyes follow your right hand moving to the rear with your line of sight in the crease of your hand (between your pointer finger and your thumb).

4 – Your arms slowly drop downward toward your body and knees slightly bend upon exhaling the breath.

Breathing Exercises | 53

5 - As your arms slowly drop towards your body, turn your hips back to the front. Perform six repetitions turning to the right side.

6 – The same procedure is followed moving to the left side of your body. The hands remain relaxed and raise up to your face area while breathing in slowly and controlled.

7 – Turning to your left on the second set of six repetitions. Looking this time through the webbing of your left hand.

8 – Slowly lower your center of gravity along with the lowering of your arms while you control your exhale of breath.

9 – Return to the starting position for the next repetition of this exercise with hands at your sides and knees slightly bent. Repeat for six repetitions turning to the left. Conduct three gathering breath repetitions when finished with this movement.

Breathing Movement #3 - Swimming Dragon (6 repetitions)

1 – Start with the same position as the first two breathing exercises.

2 – Bring your hands to the sides of your hips while bending slightly at the knees with a slight lean forward.

3 – Bending slightly more bring your hands in front of you and begin a swimming breaststroke motion while inhaling slowly.

4 – With arms now fully extended begin to circle your hands back towards your body. All motions are slow and deliberate.

5 – Continue circling your hands back towards your hips.

6 – When your hands come back to your hips, straighten your torso and turn your palms upward as if you're lifting a box in front of you. Again, all motions remain slow and deliberate.

7 – From this point, the exercise mirrors the gathering breath exercise (exercise #1). Hands circle outward and up to your head area.

8 – The hands continue circling upward while your torso rises with your inhale by straightening your knees, but never fully locking out.

9 – When hands meet at the top, you slowly lower your hands down in front of your while exhaling, slowing and lowering your torso by bending your knees slightly.

10 – Continue lowering your hands and slowly exhaling while keeping all motions slow and controlled.

11 – End with hands in front of you at your chi center (two inches below your navel). After six repetitions, perform three gathering breath movements.

Breathing Movement #4 – Carry the Ball (6 repetitions to each side)

1 – Start in the same position as the previous breathing exercises.

2 – Begin turning to your right and bring your left arm up slowly towards head level.

3 – When your left hand reaches head level, your right hand forms a cupping position just below belt level. Imagine holding a large ball and begin to turn your torso to the left.

4 – Continue turning to the left with your hands in the same position. Your arms and torso move at the same slow, deliberate speed.

5 – Exhale slowly on the rotation to your left.

6 – As you near the completion of the rotation, begin to slowly shift your hand positions so now the right hand will be at the top of the ball and your left will be on the bottom.

Breathing Exercises | 61

7 – Continue the slow, deliberate movement of switching the positioning of the hands around the imaginary ball. At this point you will begin to slowly inhale another breath.

8 – Once your hands complete the switch, begin to turn your torso back to your right and both hands will come up in front of your shoulder area side-by-side.

9 – Both hands slowly come up to the shoulder/face level. The palms will face the floor.

10 – Move slowly and deliberately throughout the breathing exercise. Arms and torso move in tandem during the turning portion of the exercise. You are focused on carrying your chi from one side to the next.

11 – Remain relaxed. Palms of your hands face the floor. Knees remain slightly bent.

12 – As you near completion of the turn, your left hand will remain up at face level and your right hand will drop down to just below the waist and cup your right hand as if you're holding a large ball again.

Breathing Exercises | 63

13 – The motions repeat for a total of six repetitions. Repeat the same motions but for six repetitions going in the opposite direction: carrying the ball from left to right, followed by carrying your chi from right to left. After completing six repetitions, perform three gathering breath movements.

Breathing Movement #5 – Upper / Middle / Lower (6 repetitions at each level)

1 – Same starting position as the other breathing exercises.

2 – Bring hands up to face area with fingertips nearly touching. Relax the arms at all times.

3 – Inhale slowly while opening the arms out to the sides of your body. As you breathe in slightly raise your torso.

Breathing Exercises | 65

4 – Slowly exhale and bring your hands back inward to the starting position. Complete six repetitions of this movement.

5 – Same movements apply but this time the starting position is in front of your torso (middle).

6 – Open up the arms to the sides of your body and inhale slowly while moving slowly and deliberately. Then exhale slowly and bring your hands back to the starting position (photo not shown). Perform six repetitions.

7 – Finally, start with your hands in front of you just below the waist with the fingertips nearly touching. This is the lower position.

8 – Inhale slowly while your arms come upward and out to the sides and raise your torso slightly. All motions and breathing are in tandem. Slowly exhale and lower your arms back to the starting point (photo not shown). Repeat for six repetitions. Conclude with three gathering breath movements.

Of particular note for all five of the breathing movements, you want to think about carrying your chi, or energy. Let your wrists and fingers hang and relax. There should be absolutely no tension in your hands, fingers, arms, legs, and so forth. There are additional thoughts to keep in mind while performing the breathing movements presented here as passed along from Master Aston Hugh from the Liuhebafa system.

2019 L-R: Master Aston Hugh, Master John McDonald, Grandmaster Isham Latimer, Master John Costanzo

Remember, where the mind goes the body will follow. When proper breathing is coupled with consistent practice, the effects will become evident in your movements and application of the Chi-Ryu Jiujitsu techniques. Over time, Chi-Ryu Jiujitsu practitioners should reflect upon additional thoughts during the practice of the breathing exercises. Those additional thoughts include:

- Two Points Breathing – think of the palms of your hands as your nostrils when inhaling and exhaling.
- Three Points Breathing – add to the Two Points Breathing the thought of the center of your forehead as your 'third eye.'
- Five Points Breathing – add to the Three Points breathing thoughts that the bottoms of your feet are also circulating the chi energy in and out of your body.
- Frog Breathing – this is when you consciously think of every cell within your body as you are breathing.
- Marrow Washing – the focus of the mind here is thinking of your bone marrow which produces healthy and fresh blood into your circulatory system. Envision this process actually happening during your breathing movements.

All of these additional thoughts that we should begin to incorporate into the breathing exercises speaks to the process of interoception, especially the 'marrow washing' thought described above. Interoception is described in Wim Hof's book *The Wim Hof Method* as "an awareness of what's going on within our bodies. Just as there are proprioceptors in our muscles and joints that detect movement, so, too, are there receptors in our internal organs, including our skin, that signal their functionality to the brain." An exercise in Hof's book to heighten your sensitivity to interoception explains, "Visualize the exchange of gases in your body. Visualize oxygen going from the lungs, through the capillaries and into the blood, and visualize the excretion of carbon dioxide upon exhalation." This is the same frame of mind and process to which Chi-Ryu Jiujitsu tries to execute in the bulleted points above while conducting the breathing exercises.

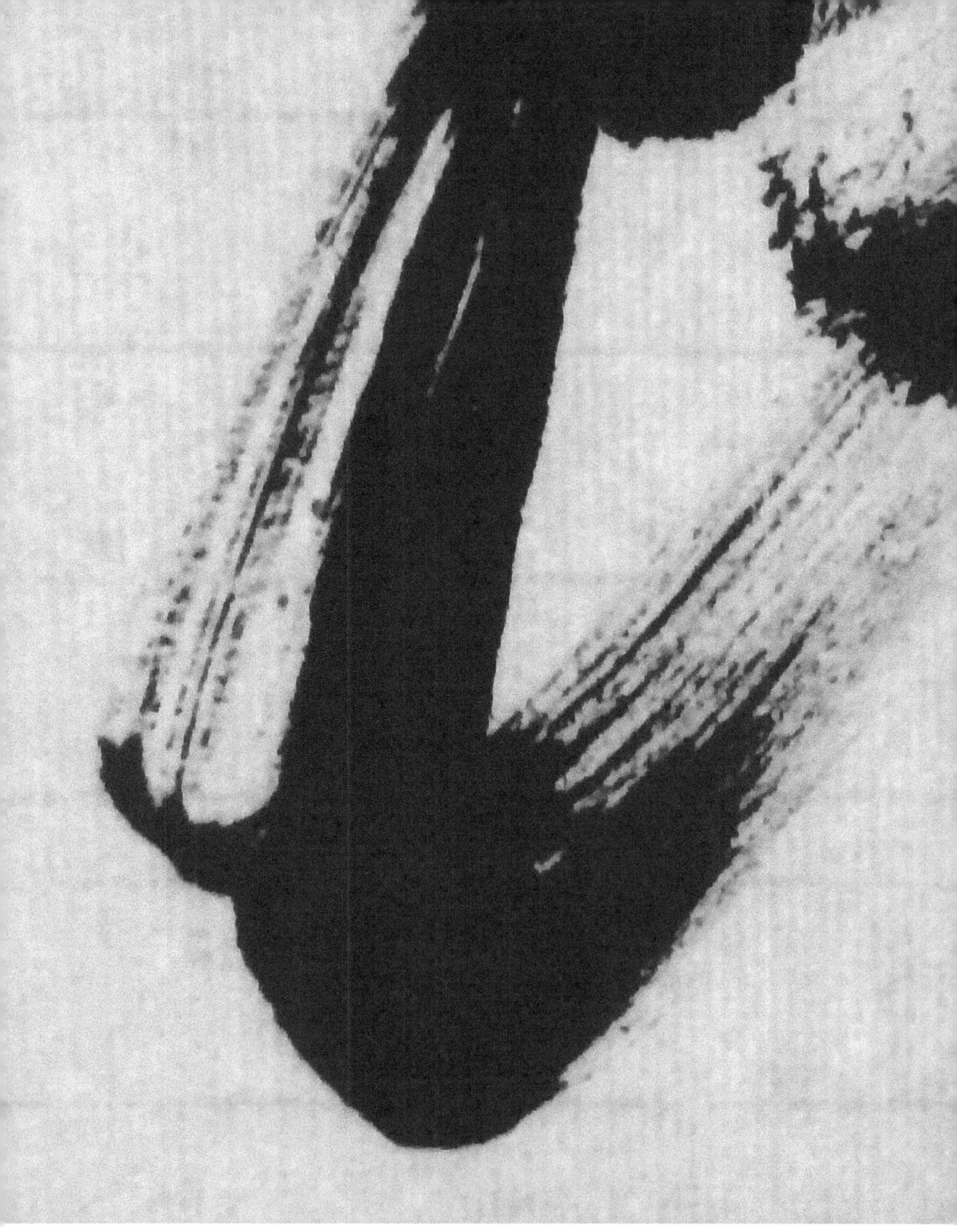

MIXXING

CHAPTER 5

"A tense muscle is equal to a closed mind."
- Grandmaster Isham Latimer

For Chi-Ryu Jiujitsu practitioners, the initial pathway to the unification of mind, body, and breath is realized and cultivated through the exercise of MiXXiNG. This exercise, developed by Grandmaster Latimer, is for the purpose of establishing and developing the practitioner's sensitivity and natural response to the physical energies and rhythmic, internal expression emanating from their training partner. The development of natural, spontaneous movement can then be applied to an actual opponent in a self-defense scenario.

Martial arts training forces practitioners to search for weaknesses in his or her opponent's power and defenses. As such, the martial arts practitioner must have the ability to change according to the situation. There also needs to be a general awareness of the concepts of leverage, coiling, turning, slanting, triangulation, friction, balance of power, and the opposition of forces. These concepts are crucial to the development of one's appropriate physical, emotional, and natural or intuitive responses to an opposing physical force. How that force may be best controlled and developed is by the practice of this exercise.

While engaging in MiXXiNG, the student must maintain continual contact with his or her training partner. This approach simulates close quarter combat situations in a dynamic and functional way and increases the practitioner's balance, perception, and ability to anticipate or sense when their opponent's energy changes or resets in its movement. All contact is performed in a smooth, brushing motion and coordinated with the training partner's forearms, hands, wrists, and shoulders while continually using your stances and footwork to keep the motion continuous.

When you observe two Chi-Ryu practitioners engaged in the MiXXiNG drill who have a good command of their movement, you begin to notice a common thread: All motion tends to come back to the center. As Master Costanzo puts it, "There is a pyramid of movement where everything meets at the top."

The following sequences are just a portion of the MiXXiNG drill but they reveal several commonalities: continuous contact, relaxed postures as evidenced by the open hands, and continuous movement. (Photos move from left to right)

Contact is maintained at all times and the arms continuously move in all directions without usage of strength but rather controlled breathing.

Without reliance upon muscular strength, the drill can continue for quite some time without losing one's breath or needing to stop. The objective is to move and react based on the opponent's motion and not worry about striking or being hit.

When executed as intended, this sensitivity drill can reveal the partner's chi energy to which you want to maintain harmony in motion rather than fight against your opponent.

As the motion of the right hand from Grandmaster Latimer (on right) comes forward, Master Costanzo, on the left, gently redirects the energy to the side as shown in the sequence above and below.

Chi-Ryu Jiujitsu

The sequences above and below show Grandmaster Latimer's circular arm motions to keep the drill continuously moving. Notice the shifting of the feet and stances in tandem with the arm movements.

MiXXiNG can also present defensive opportunities that can apply to actual self-defense. The following sequence shows the flow from initial engagement progressing into an inside wrist joint lock by Master McDonald on the left.

The circular motion allows Master McDonald to naturally turn his left hand while connected to Master Costanzo's right hand, and then catch the hand into a wrist lock when the circular motion moves from outside to inside. The following photos show this sequence of motion in close up:

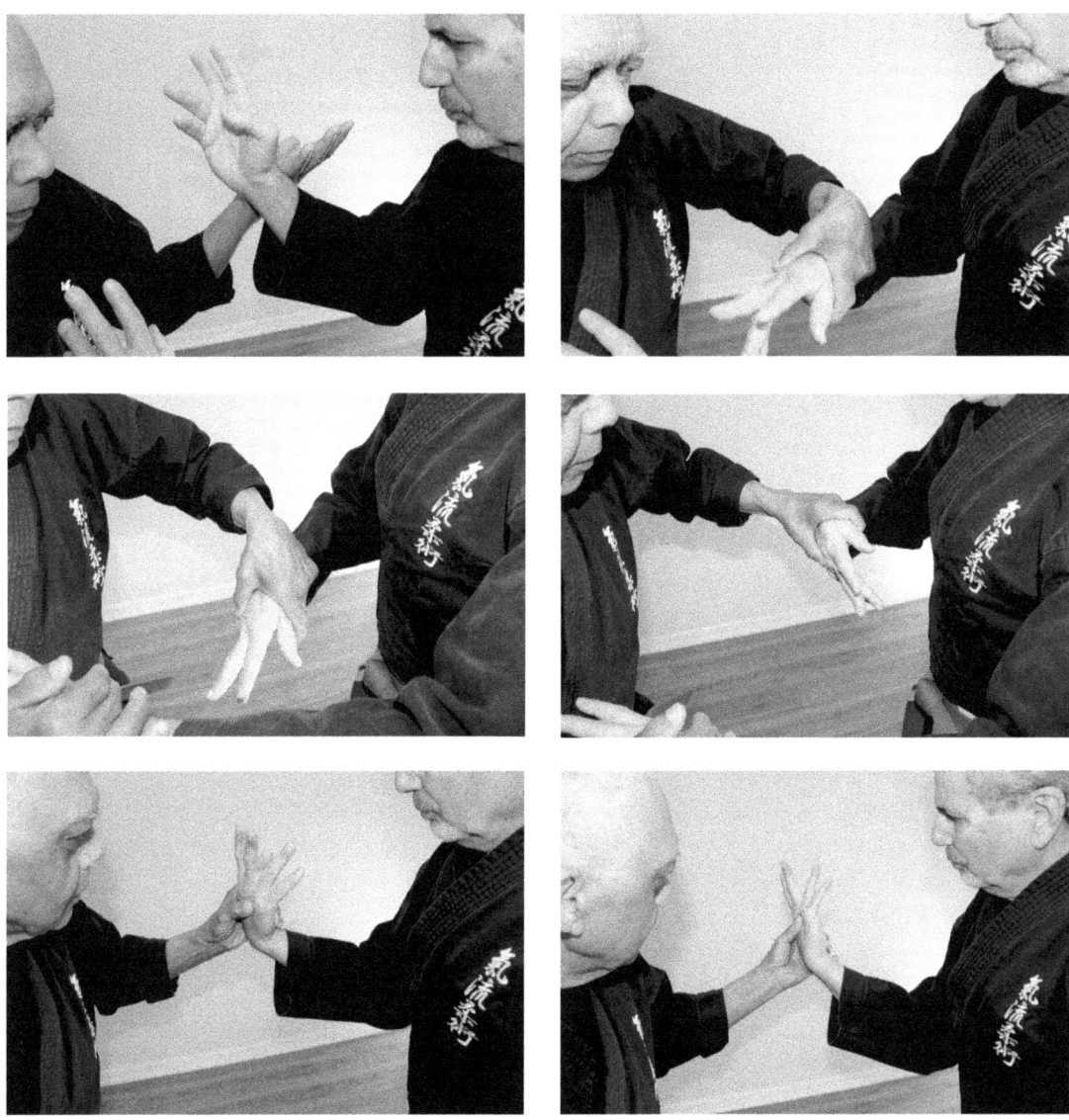

The idea in MiXXiNG is to lose your ego and sense of stopping, starting, winning or losing. Allow yourself to be absorbed by the approaching energy or movement, and simultaneously guide that same energy to a place where it has no effect on you. Your body must be free of muscle tension as well as heavy thoughts of accomplishing the small-minded goals such as striking, blocking and dominating. Rather, the focus should be on the greater purpose of coordination of mind, body, and breath through deep, controlled breathing along with slow and continuous fluid movements utilizing the concept and method of "one thing moves, everything moves."

The idea of slower movement should be a critical point of reference here. There is a saying: *Slow is smooth, smooth is fast, fast is deadly.* This concept applies in almost every area of life. When things get out of control…slow down. The author Norman Vincent Peale tells the following story in his book *The Power of Positive Thinking,* "A former member of a championship university crew [rowing] told me that their shrewd crew coach often reminded them: "To win this or any race, row slowly." He pointed out that rapid rowing tends to break the stroke and when the stroke is broken it is with the greatest difficulty that the crew recovers the rhythm necessary to win. Meanwhile other crews pass the disorganized group. It is indeed wise advice – "To go fast, row slowly." This is precisely what the MiXXiNG drill of Chi-Ryu Jiujitsu tries to convey.

Slower movement allows for an appropriate response to those changes felt during the MiXXiNG drill which would include a locking technique, a reversal of movement to confuse the opponent, or a motion that follows the opponent's retreating motion thus allowing a counter strike or attack. The drill stimulates visualization, which enables you to find endless paths of recovery from opposing forces or attacks. During the exercise, constant contact is maintained by smoothly brushing and coordinating with the partner's forearms, hands, wrists, shoulders, and all other areas, though it is primarily focused on the entire arm and points of the shoulders.

Over time and with a sufficient degree of comfort with the drill, you can then add some personal concepts and see how your training partner reacts. For example, you can 'lead' the motions in a specific direction, such as slightly to the side of the shoulder, to determine if the other person will follow. This would be similar to a fake in boxing but at a pace on par with the MiXXiNG drill requirements. Another example would be figuring out the optimal 'set up' or sequence of motions to get your training partner turned into a position that would enable a push or similar motion to off-balance the other person. Essentially, your MiXXiNG practice will begin to subconsciously add definitive defensive tactics without any thoughts or effort on your part. They will flow into the movement of the drill naturally.

Over time, you will slowly increase your coordination and chi energy levels through breathing that coordinates with the movements of your entire body. Those movements must be slow, fluid, and continuous. Practice this exercise regularly and you will begin to understand your biomechanics more, to the point where you are performing the drill with a relaxed body and never becoming static and easily countered.

With ongoing practice of MiXXiNG, you will begin to see your energy increasing as the coordination of your mind, body and breath increases. You'll notice you can perform the drill for long periods of time without tiring from muscle tension or mental anxiety or stress. The intent of the drill is to develop or achieve *mushin*, or the state of 'no mind' where reaction is relied upon and with no intentional thought on how to react. In other words, instinct of movement will begin to take over as you become egoless and softer in your motions thus allowing you to observe and process, subconsciously, the movements of your training partner, giving you a greater anticipation of their movements without thought.

MOVEMENTS OF CHI-RYU JIUJITSU

CHAPTER 6

"Because movement is everywhere. Even in immobility."

- Artist Luo Li Rong

The Chi-Ryu Jiujitsu curriculum includes the accumulation of *movements*, or short patterns of defensive techniques against a variety of attacking methods. The term movement most clearly defines the concept of all skills and techniques as being open and flowing, where there is continuous flow of energy and motion. The idea behind Chi-Ryu Jiujitsu movements is there are no boundaries in the performance of any technique. The movements should have the ability to utilize circular motion and continual flow of energy or *chi*. The MiXXiNG drill described and demonstrated in the previous chapter serves as a basis for the execution of the various Chi-Ryu Jiujitsu movements.

At present there are 30 movements taught within the Chi-Ryu Jiujitsu system. The movements of Chi-Ryu Jiujitsu training provide a basis and foundation for the forms that students must learn in order to progress through the various ranks. Japanese and Okinawan systems of martial arts call their forms *kata*, Korean systems use the terms *hyeong, pumsae* or *teul*, and Chinese systems refer to *Tao Lu* when speaking of prearranged forms. Of note, the first five movements learned in Chi-Ryu Jiujitsu comprise one of the initial forms of the system, called Circle Form. Therefore, the presentation of the movements in this chapter will include a sampling of six of the overall 30 total movements.

The movements are meant to introduce you to various key concepts and techniques so you can practice them repeatedly until they become natural and fluid. This practice will help you develop control over your movement, breathing, and techniques. Generally speaking, when responding to a physical or emotional attack, the mind becomes rushed and the physical body tends to become rigid, heavy, or weighted. Those conditions minimize your ability to respond efficiently, and it also interferes with your breathing and the ability to adapt or adjust in the most fluid and effective manner. This is a big concept within the martial art of Aikido. In Gaku Homma's book *Aikido for Life* he explains, "When the physical and psychological elements of an exercise are harmonized, your strength and energy are amplified several times." The physical element is controlled by relaxing the mind and by not relying upon muscle. Rather, you need to use the natural structures of your body to move efficiently. The psychological element is controlled with proper breathing. When combined properly, your movements and reactions will have plenty of strength to handle the needs at the moment. There is no reason to tense your muscles to move properly in a defense situation.

The movements of Chi-Ryu Jiujitsu are short sequences intended to develop better control over breathing, technique, and relaxation. The movements must be performed with the body being properly connected, rounded, and balanced. You will realize quickly during practice of MiXXiNG that if those three components are not in sync, you will lose your balance, and your breathing will be tight and labored. These movements must be controlled in order to remain effective with your techniques. Always remember that how you train is how you will react when necessary.

The Chi-Ryu Jiujitsu student is introduced early in their training to the internal system of Liuhebafa, which means six coordinations or harmonies (Liu He) achieved through eight methods (Ba Fa). Six harmonies pertain to unification of the body, while the eight methods concern practical applications. The six coordinations include: body and mind, mind and intention, intention and chi, chi and spirit, spirit and movement, and movement and emptiness. The eight methods are: chi, bone, shape, follow, rise, return, retain, and conceal. All of these concepts lead to the ability to change according to the situation. This ability to change, as needed, can only be accomplished when the main joints of the body start together and stop together in harmony. The movements one learns in Chi-Ryu Jiujitsu provide a short scenario where the student can practice bringing all movement of the body into harmony for optimum effect of technique.

Ready Postures

There are generally two main ready postures or stances for Chi-Ryu Jiujitsu. One of these postures is demonstrated in the sample of movements shown later in this chapter. The other one is presented for reference to demonstrate the variance between a self-defense ready posture for Chi-Ryu Jiujitsu versus one used in a typical karate style of martial arts.

The natural posture shown here is reflected in the movement samples within this chapter. With this posture, you are fully relaxed and both hands are open in front of your waist. This is where many agree chi energy is stored within the body and flows from this area to all parts of the body. In this posture, you can easily conceal a bladed weapon from the potential adversary as well, if needed.

The other ready posture (shown below) for Chi-Ryu Jiujitsu is the typical guard position that many systems of martial arts contain. Generally, the stance requires the arms up and hands closed into a fist ready to punch. For Chi-Ryu Jiujitsu, the arms are up but the hands remain open and relaxed with the palms facing inward. Also, the arms are in a circular position that stems from one of the eight principles of Liuhebafa: structure. This circular structure facilitates the muscles to relax and the chi energy to remain flowing and not shut off by angular positions. This keeps the energy of the body within your circle, which provides the strength needed to block in incoming strike. The relaxed and open hands facilite an immediate controlling movement of the incoming striking limb. This structure goes hand-in-hand with the *gathering breath* drill provided in chapter 4.

Blocking Structure

Within the various movements, you will notice quite a few blocks immediately become a striking technique. Many traditional systems of karate block with one hand, and counterattack with the other hand. This appears to be more or less a process to teach students how to execute the striking movements of the arms. In reality, both hands need to be used simultaneously in a continuous motion to be effective. The blocking hand needs to be able to switch to attacking sequences immediately. Or, the non-blocking hand needs to deploy its counterattack nearly simultaneously with the block. In other words, the blocking hand should switch between blocking and attacking in an instant, where the rear hand could jam, strike or grab at any time. Blocking and then countering with the same arm was considered true bujutsu to famed Okinawan karate master Choki Motobu. In addition, many of the hand movements lead to continuous movement and joint locking techniques, stemming from Chin Na techniques and applications.

Two differences in blocking techniques between traditional martial arts and Chi-Ryu Jiujitsu are demonstrated below. For a parrying type of block or deflection in traditional karate (photo on left), the arm used tends to be very rigid with the blocking forearm vertical in orientation to the punch. With the fist of the blocking arm clenched it is challenging to remain relaxed both during and immediately after the parry of the incoming attack.

For blocks or parries within the movements of Chi-Ryu Jiujitsu (photo on right), you should remain relaxed for an appropriate response and let the body mechanics do the work. If the attack is some type of grabbing attempt or a straight in stabbing attack with a knife, your parry should be performed with the arm in a slight angle, the body remaining relaxed, and redirecting the attack towards the inside of your body. Notice the hand of the parrying arm is open and relaxed allowing for a smooth transition from the parry to either a grab or an open hand strike with the same hand. The opposite hand is also much higher and closer to the action allowing for a quicker counter movement as opposed to being on the hip, which is common for traditional karate as shown in the photo on the left.

The figure on the left below shows a traditional karate side block technique against a straight punch. Again, the fist of the blocking arm is clenched and causes a degree of tension. The opposite fist is on the hip of the defender, which is commonly taught in traditional karate systems.

If we consider the typical attack on the street today, punching attacks tend to be in a roundhouse motion. In those situations, a traditional karate block would be less effective as the punch would circle around the structure of the blocking arm. In the case of a common roundhouse attack, Chi-Ryu Jiujitsu utilizes a circular structure of the arm to meet the attack on the plane that it is traveling as shown in the photo above to the right. Notice the hand of the blocking arm is open and relaxed. There is no need for conscious use of power on the defender's side as the attacker is providing all the power. The circular structure of the blocking arm provides all that is needed to stop the attack. The open hand of the blocking arm allows for an immediate transition from block to control using your hand. Again, notice the opposite (right) hand is off the hip and prepared for an immediate counterattack technique.

The following series of photos demonstrates the immediate transition from the Chi-Ryu Jiujitsu blocking method into a control of the attacker's punching arm:

Above all, you must have a strong, controlled structure while performing all movements. Remaining relaxed and moving deliberately with controlled breathing is paramount to a strong foundation for defense. A weak, or structurally flawed posture will limit the amount of power you can deliver. This structure doesn't necessarily require massive amounts of muscle to control. What is required are: sound stances, proper breathing, positioning of the limbs and joints as described with the incoming roundhouse punch, and a proper combination of relaxation and tension of the muscles. Proper connection of breathing to movement is of absolute necessity in order for power transfer of the entire body and continual endurance of movement. When this level is achieved, the use of power appears to be without effort.

The movements learned and practiced as the basics to the Chi-Ryu Jiujitsu system require an internal calmness, even though you are physically moving. This stems from the Liuhebafa internal system and takes considerable time and repetition to get comfortable with. The level to which practitioners of Chi-Ryu Jiujitsu aspire is the state of emptiness, or *wu-ji*. Wu-ji is the point of quiet, motionless state achieved when your movement follows the body's automatic reaction to a given situation or circumstance. As Grandmaster Latimer states often, "You are where you are, now work from there." The ability to adapt, change movement, and remain calm in order to effectively distribute the proper level of energy behind your defensive techniques is the goal behind Chi-Ryu Jiujitsu. The 30 movements are the hinge upon which to work towards meeting those goals.

Another key to the purpose of learning the various movements and continual repetition of them is to develop space awareness and understanding just how close the opponent is to you. Distance is your friend; however, techniques become effective when you are close to the opponent which, allows you to control their limbs and a much quicker delivery of your techniques. In time, the aim of practicing the movements is to pick up information or signals from the opponent before you are consciously aware of it. Your intent is to acquire sensitivity and flow of your movement. You will also notice one of the underlying themes of Chi-Ryu Jiujitsu movements is to disorient the attacker as quickly as possible. This involves striking to the head or neck area in order to immediately stun the attacker and thus enhance your overall effectiveness.

To improve your breathing, which is of paramount importance, into effective execution of the movements and forms of Chi-Ryu Jiujitsu, you must always go back to the previous chapters on breathing and MiXXiNG. The material presented there is the foundation upon which Chi-Ryu Jiujitsu stands. Without continual practice of those concepts it will be quite difficult to grasp and properly execute the overall essence of the concept – *when one thing moves, everything moves*. Therefore, the practice of breathing must become a daily part of your routine.

Don't be fooled about the need to practice your breathing. You might think the process of breathing is already understood; however, it's the *control* of your breathing that is the key. Regardless of your situation, control over your breath is essential to a relaxed mind. This is the case for any athletic participation and especially in the event of a self-defense situation. Take a look at any sport such as baseball, football, golf, or tennis. When the results are not good, the athlete tends to look tense due to lack of control over their breathing. Think of any top athlete from past or present and you'll notice they appear relaxed, as if they're hardly breathing with any effort. This is not by accident. Those athletes have practiced situational breathing enough to know that controlling their breath is essential to performance at a level which they envision.

Breathing in tandem with movement is paramount to learning control over your breathing. The breathing exercises described previously allow you to focus on both elements of breathing and movement as they are performed slowly and deliberately. When it comes to standard speeds of motion, a more deliberate awareness on breathing is needed. Everything requires proper breath control. Even with activities such as distance running. If your breathing is out of sync with your motions, then your running technique cannot improve. Proper breathing leads to relaxed, controlled movement – leading to improvement of that movement. The same mindset is needed for the sound execution of techniques for training in the Chi-Ryu Jiujitsu system.

SAMPLE MOVEMENTS OF CHI-RYU JIUJITSU

Movement #3 – Defense Against Front Punch or Grab

Demonstrated by Master John Costanzo

The attacker prepares to strike. Notice defender's hands are in front of the body, open and relaxed and not held in tight fists. This allows for a natural, spontaneous reaction to a strike, grab, push, or other type of attack.

Attacker attempts a front punch (could be a grab). Defender lowers bodyweight slightly and performs an open hand deflecting block downward.

Attacker quickly attempts a roundhouse punch with left arm to the face. Defender stops the force of the punch with an open hand block while keeping the arm in a rounded position. Notice there is not a wide or deep stance by the Defender in this situation as it is not needed. The structure of the blocking arm allows for Defender to remain relaxed and still have the ability to stop the incoming roundhouse punch by Attacker.

Once the previous block is performed, Defender immediately turns the right blocking hand around to control the Attacker's wrist. This is immediately followed by Defender performing a knife hand strike with the left hand to Attacker's ribs and simultaneously performing a stomping kick with the right foot to Attacker's knee.

After the knife hand strike and stomping kick are executed, Defender maintains control of Attacker's left arm and steps through with his left foot to prepare for a sweeping technique.

Once Defender steps through with his left foot, he ensures that his right foot is placed between Attacker's feet. Notice the back of Defender's right leg is now firmly placed against Attacker's left knee area.

Defender now applies an arm bar motion to Attacker's left arm while also performing a sweeping motion with his right leg in order to unbalance Attacker and send his body forward to the ground.

Defender completes the technique by maintaining control over Attacker's hand.

Movement #4 – Defense Against Roundhouse Punch

Demonstrated by Grandmaster Isham Latimer

Defender remains relaxed with hands open in front of his midsection.

Attacker attempts a roundhouse punch to Defender's head region. Defender executes a block by keeping his hand open and his arm in a rounded structure. Defender's opposite hand is in front of him, open and relaxed allowing it to remain ready to react quickly to another attacking motion.

Attacker attempts a second punching attack to Defender's center mass region. Defender executes an inward deflecting block while his left hand controls Attacker's wrist. Notice Defender's hand with his blocking arm remains open to facilitate quick reaction and possible controlling techniques.

After the inside deflection block, Defender now goes on the offensive and shuffles forward to strike Attacker's neck area with a knife hand strike with his right hand.

The sequence above and below show Defender controlling Attacker's wrist after the inward deflection block. When Defender shuffles closer to Attacker, notice how Attacker's wrist is now fully controlled by bending the wrist and Defender using his body as the base for Attacker's elbow.

The picture above shows Attacker's left wrist is now fully controlled and Defender executing the throat strike. This strike is a follow-through motion that sets up the distance for the next elbow strike as shown in the next photo.

Defender performs an elbow strike to Attacker's head region while still maintaining control over Attacker's left arm. After the elbow strike, Defender extends his own arm to create an imbalance in Attacker's stance and position as shown below.

Defender executes a knee strike to Defender's lower back region

Defender then performs a backward take-down technique and controls Attacker as shown below.

Movement #8 – Defense Against Front Grab

Demonstrated by Master John Costanzo

Defender prepares for an attack and remains calm with hands open and prepared for a quick reaction.

Attacker attempts a front grab. Defender quickly moves in with left foot to close the gap and prepare to deflect the attack.

Defender parries Attacker's left hand and simultaneously performs palm heel strike to the Attacker's jaw.

Defender quickly wraps up Attacker's right arm to maintain control after the palm strike and brings his right arm from the prior deflection block down and into a ridge hand strike to Attacker's groin region.

After the ridge hand strike with right hand, Defender grabs whatever is available and pulls Attacker in while executing a left elbow strike to Attacker's head region.

Continuing the flowing motion, Defender then brings his right hand up and overtop to deliver a ridge hand strike to Attacker's neck region.

Close up of the finished ridge hand strike to the neck region of Attacker.

Defender then controls Attacker's head with his left hand and turns Attacker's head to the inside. Notice there is no space between Defender's body and Attacker's head. Defender's body serves as a base to control the head of Attacker.

Defender then quickly turns Attacker's head to the outside with both hands to finish off Attacker and move him out of the way.

Movement #9 – Defense Against a Roundhouse Punch

Demonstrated by Master John McDonald

Defender faces Attacker in relaxed stance with hands open and prepared for quick reaction to any potential movement.

Attacker attempts roundhouse punch. Defender intercepts the punch and simultaneously begins to deliver a whipping backfist strike to Attacker's head region.

Reverse angle showing Defender's backfist strike to Attacker's head region.

Defender executes a downward strike to Attacker's initial punching arm to unbalance Attacker slightly. Defender's right hand will immediately control the same arm leading into a follow-up strike with his left hand.

As noted previously, Attacker's initial punching arm is now controlled and Defender turns his torso and executes a knife hand strike to Attacker's side/front neck region that follows through the target area.

From the neck strike, Defender uses same arm and performs a downward elbow strike to Attacker's arm around the elbow joint region. Notice Defender's hand is open during the elbow strike. This allows Defender to continue his process of controlling Attacker's arm after the strike as show below.

Defender continues to wrap up Attacker's arm after the previous elbow strike and simultaneously executes an open-handed throat strike with his right hand.

The throat strike is followed by an upward palm heel strike to Attacker's chin to disorient Attacker further. This allows Defender to prepare for a leg sweep takedown as shown with Defender's right foot beginning to step behind Attacker's stance.

Defender begins the takedown by combining his right foot position between Attacker's legs and the push/pull pressure of right hand at chin level (push) and controlling Attacker's right arm with his left arm.

Reverse angle just prior to the takedown. Notice Defender's right foot position is between Attacker's stance, his left arm is wrapping up Attacker's arm, and Attacker's vision is distorted from the palm heel strike to the chin.

Follow through and finish of the take down for movement #9.

Movement #15 – Defense Against Front Grab Attempt

Demonstrated by Grandmaster Isham Latimer

Attacker begins front side attack by attempting to grab Defender who is in a relaxed stance with hands open and prepared for quick reaction.

Defender intercepts the attempted grab and deflects Attacker's hands upward. Notice Defender's arms are rounded to create a strong structure in which to prevent the grab.

Defender immediately performs a palm heel strike with his left hand to Attacker's head region to disorient Attacker. Notice Defender's right hand is withdrawing slightly to prepare for a similar strike in a one-two immediate combination.

Defender follows up with right hand palm heel strike to Attacker's head region while also controlling Attacker's right arm at the wrist. Notice Defender moved in slightly.

Defender follows-up from the palm heel strike with his right hand and drops his center of gravity into a punch to Attacker's upper leg region. Notice Defender maintains control over Attacker's arm during the punching technique.

From the punch to Attacker's upper leg, Defender brings his arm upward to hyperextend Attacker's arm which Defender is still maintaining control.

Defender then turns his torso to his right (this is a reverse angle) and switches the hand controlling Attacker at the wrist (right hand is now controlling instead of the left at the wrist). Defender continues to hyperextend Attacker's arm by striking to Attacker's neck region and then hooking his left hand to control Attacker's neck.

Defender applies a knee strike to Attacker's elbow while maintaining control with the hooking technique to the neck region.

From there Defender steps inward with his left foot and ducks underneath Attacker's arm. Defender continues circling by then stepping back with his right foot.

Defender completes the step back with his right foot and begins to control Attacker's hand/wrist with both hands to prepare for a takedown.

Defender continues to turn Attacker's hand/wrist to the outside which facilitates the takedown.

Attacker falls to the ground and Defender locks Attacker's arm to ensure full control of the situation.

Movement #19 – Defense Against Grab From the Back

Demonstrated by Master John McDonald

It must be noted that many of the techniques and movements within the Chi-Ryu Jiujitsu system are interchangeable. The idea is for smooth reaction and flowing movement very similar to that of the Filipino martial arts systems. This is a big reason for the inclusion of Modern Arnis into the overall Chi-Ryu Jiujitsu system. For the following Movement #19, Master McDonald demonstrates an alternate technique from that typically taught.

Defender is grabbed from the rear on his shoulder (note: the technique works if grabbed on either shoulder).

Defender seizes Attacker's hand for control and begins to turn his torso.

The turn continues and Defender performs elbow strike with his left elbow. The technique's motion continues past Attacker's head region into an arm wrap/control of Attacker's arm that grabbed initially. Notice Defender's right hand still maintains control over Attacker's hand that grabbed at the start of the defensive technique.

Reverse angle of the follow through after the elbow strike previously. Defender is beginning to wrap up Attacker's arm at the elbow joint with his left arm.

Defender now executes another elbow strike to the head region after Attacker's right arm is fully controlled. The spacing is very close between Attacker and Defender.

After the previous elbow to the head region, Defender now applies a figure-four control over Attacker's arm in preparation for a takedown.

Reverse angle showing the figure-four control of Attacker's arm.

Defender steps through and behind Attacker's stance and performs a takedown of Attacker.

LIUHEBAFA

CHAPTER 7

" Destroy hard force with soft strength[1]"

Introduction to the System

Liuhebafa, meaning Six Harmonies Eight Methods, is a considerable part of the study and research within the Chi-Ryu Jiujitsu system. Six Harmonies pertain to the unification of the body, while Eight Methods refer to practical applications of the techniques. This discipline was developed in China by Chen Xi Yi (c.871-989 A.D.). He was known for his advanced theories on philosophical Taoism, Buddhism and Confucianism. "Xi" is what cannot be heard; "Yi" is what cannot be seen[2]. Also known by the name Chen Tuan, he was a pioneer of the internal forms of martial arts. Chen was a Taoist sage at the beginning of the Song Dynasty (960-1279[3]). The actual name of the style is "Hua Yue Xi Yi Men," whereas Liuhebafa is merely a description of the principles involved.[4]

The system is sometimes referred to as Water Boxing. This is derived from the nature of water in that water can alter its state to become ice (solid state), water (liquid state), and steam (gaseous state). Liuhebafa's water principle is based on these three characteristics giving birth to structured strength (solid) and ceaseless flow (liquid), both components being contained within emptiness (gas)[5]. Structured strength comes internally from your tendons and bones, and not from the muscles. The liquid state, or continuous flow, can only happen if your mind and body are appropriately

---

1 The Five Word Poem of LiuHeBaFa, by Hui Kit Wah, Stuart Agars, Ruth Hampson. Principle #30
2 Liuhebafa Chuan – The 4th Internal Art, by Nomura Akihiko. Hiden Budo & Bujutsu Magazine (Japan)
3 https://en.wikipedia.org/wiki/Song_dynasty
4 Liuhebafa Chuan – The 4th Internal Art, by Nomura Akihiko. Hiden Budo & Bujutsu Magazine (Japan)
5 Liuhebafa Chuan – The 4th Internal Art, by Nomura Akihiko. Hiden Budo & Bujutsu Magazine (Japan)

relaxed and working in tandem with proper breathing. When the structure and flow of the body are working together and the muscles remain relaxed, the martial artist realizes Liuhebafa begins to reveal that there is another level or layer to your skills of defense.

The liquid state which leads to the usage of the term Water Boxing cannot be overstated. Everyone has heard the legendary Bruce Lee's words, "Be like water, my friend." The longer version is Lee explaining how water cannot be contained, how it molds to whatever container you place it in, as well as how powerful water can be. He most likely garnered these words from the *I Ching* and its principles. Da Liu explains in his book *Tai Chi Chuan and I Ching* the events leading up to the formulation of Tai Chi Chuan by Chang San-feng. Chang observed a fight between a snake and a crane and noticed how both animals would apply the concept of yielding in the face of strength. Liu writes, "He [Chang San-feng] saw in living form the principle of the *I Ching*: the strong changing to the yielding and the yielding changing to the strong. He then remembered the teaching: 'What is more yielding than water? Yet [water] comes back to wear down the stone.'" Liuhebafa has at its core this concept of being like water and yielding when necessary. Considering how water always seems to come back, is it any wonder why practitioners of Tai Chi can continue practicing well into their advanced years?

Clearly, Liuhebafa was developed a long time ago and coupled with the internal aspects of the art, the martial artist with a serious interest should conduct deep research to fully appreciate what this style has to offer. There are excellent resources available in print today that can assist with this research (see *Sources* at end of this book). Of note, Paul Dillon's book *Liuhebafa Five Character Secrets* provides a great summary of the interrelation of the Chinese systems of Liuhebafa, Xingyi, Taiji, and Bagua.

At first, my experience in training in this style showed just how tense my motions, stances, limbs and postures were at all times. Trying to follow along with the breathing exercises, the MiXXiNG drill, and learning the sequences of the Liuhebafa form seemed an infinite struggle. I would continually revert back to my karate training and experiences and try to incorporate those applications into the Liuhebafa training. This proved time and again to be frustrating as I had a difficult time relaxing and simply allowing my breathing and physical structure to handle what was needed to execute the movements correctly. The more power I tried to summon, the more tense I got and the more easily I lost control of the movements.

Over time I began to understand what was needed to move more efficiently. I needed to control and regulate my breathing and simply allow my natural physical attributes of the bones and tendons to handle how I moved. I eventually came to the realization that what Liuhebafa has to offer can take my martial arts practice to another level. I noticed how much more efficiently The Three Pillars controlled their techniques, breathing and movement from their training in Liuhebafa and knew there was something more to this than what meets the eye. I started to realize, it seems the internal aspects of the martial arts have been brushed aside by today's modern martial artist. This should warrant reflection and introspection if you wish to fully appreciate what it is you are doing and why you are training in the martial arts to begin with.

The Three Pillars are all over 70 years of age, yet they continue to seriously train because of their good health and ability to move freely. My assessment of training in Liuhebafa for over 10 years now and watching The Three Pillars, I believe a key to improved health and movement stems in large part to proper breathing. This realization has led me down other paths of research into the science of breathing correctly and how it ties into martial arts training.

The benefits of proper breathing are endless and is the foundation of Liuhebafa. The student needs to realize that coordination of mind, body and breath takes considerable time to achieve. In light of those wishing to earn their black belt within several years in many of the popular systems of today, this may be a big reason for the lack of attention provided to the internal aspects of the martial arts. People in today's world simply don't wish to invest the time necessary to fully understand the effectiveness of the internal aspects of the martial arts.

Liuhebafa has core principles and training methods not found in other martial arts. Your intention should be sharply focused on each movement, and the movements are led by your mind and intention[6]. Another of the main tenets of the system is internal strength – not from muscular power but from tendons and bones. This means the structure of the body contains everything you need to handle an attack. This internal strength is developed in Chi-Ryu Jiujitsu through the breathing exercises and the MiXXiNG drill provided in earlier chapters. You cannot understand by simply looking at Liuhebafa. You need to engage in the practice and understand from connectivity, especially with the arms, and feeling your training partner's energy.

There is also a form, called Zhu Ji, which consists of 66 movements. Zhu Ji contains no repeating movements and is performed in the spirit of proper speed found in Tai Chi. So generally speaking, the student of Liuhebafa initially must learn the correct postures of the system while over time slowly learn to cultivate internal energy through sound breathing and appropriate intentions of the mind and body in coordination with each other. Overall, one's mind, intention, spirit and chi should coordinate with external body movements.

Technique is influenced by the formal study of a particular system over time and regardless of the style, every skill or technique has one fundamental element at its genesis: movement.

With those tenets in mind, Chi-Ryu Jiujitsu's developers incorporated the training of the internal system, Hsing-I Liuhebafa Chuan and it's concept of unbroken movement coordinated with breathing for all skills development. These skills include, but are not limited to, teaching their students proper breathing techniques. This approach lends to the understanding of the concept: *when one thing moves, everything moves*.

When techniques and breathing are combined in the correct manner, energy is generated to the practitioner's benefit. As discussed by Xiaoling Liu in his article that *The Beginning of the Liu He Ba Fa Form*, "These energies are hard energy, soft energy, spinning

---

6 http://www.wudanglongmen.com/liuhebafa.html

energy, rotating energy, whipping energy, pinning energy, hooking energy, sinking energy, shaking energy, and springing energy. The change of energy includes both blocking and attacking, storing and discharging, slowing down and speeding up, and emptying out and filling in. It circles around, extends out and withdrawals, and opens and closes unpredictably."[7]

The internal arts such as Liuhebafa do not solely rely on muscle strength to be effective. Attention is also provided to development and understanding of breathing, tendons, and the body's own fascia, the fibrous connective tissue that encases our bodies below the surface of the skin. An understanding and development of using this fascia is essential for effective usage of Liuhebafa. As Christopher McDougall writes in *Natural Born Heroes*, "When it comes to raw strength, muscle is only a minority partner. The real powerhouse is our *fascia profunda*, the stretchy tissue that encases our organs and muscle." McDougall explains fascia can be fully understood from the efforts of Thomas Myers, a pioneering researcher in connective tissue. In 1999, Myers discovered much more about fascia during a cadaver dissection. By cutting out only the fascia he had "a full-length body sleeve that resembled a lumpy wetsuit. Under magnification, the fascia was so latticed, it seemed to have the tensile strength of storm netting."

Coordinating mind, breath, tendons and fascia allows the practitioner to move effortlessly with optimum effect in techniques delivered. This pertains to the liquid state of Water Boxing alluded to previously. This coordinated effort is presented in McDougall's book, which covers how the native Greeks survived the German invasion of the island of Crete during World War II. The Cretans would travel all night by foot over extremely rugged terrain to avoid capture and transmit communications among themselves. As McDougall writes in regard to optimum use of their breathing, tendons, and fascia, "Instead of struggling, they seemed to fall upward, bouncing from rock to rock for hours with an odd, effortless-looking elasticity. It wasn't just the men; Cretan women could likewise carry heftier packs, cover longer distances, navigate through snow and dark, and thrive on a diet plucked from the ground as they passed. Strength didn't explain it – it was as if the Cretans were drawing on something else, a martial art of energy mastery. Under any kind of pressure, physical or mental, they seemed to become more pliable."

The people of Crete were able to use a sort of parkour motion to their travels in order to remain in motion all night while living on a spartan diet. Parkour requires free motion that can only be accomplished with a relaxed mind and breathing coupled with reliance upon the elasticity built into the body's tendons and fascia. If muscles are overly tense, leading to fatigue, the parkour enthusiast's movement will suffer and his motion will be short-lived. They must rely on the body's natural movement and elasticity to bounce from skill to skill. The same holds true for the practitioner of Liuhebafa, who understands the recoil and bounce back strength derived from your body's own fascia.

---

[7] http://www.wudanglongmen.com/liuhebafa.html

Coupled with this elasticity is the ongoing development of calmness of the mind and breathing while moving. When all of these attributes are in unison, the enhancement and effectiveness of your defensive techniques grows substantially.

The Liuhebafa Form – An Introduction

The form for Liuhebafa taught in the Chi-Ryu Jiujitsu system takes approximately eight minutes to perform. The speed of motion observed for Tai Chi Chuan is essentially the same for Liuhebafa performance. The initial movements of the form learned for Chi-Ryu Jiujitsu are presented here. Chi-Ryu Jiujitsu students first learn the proper breathing techniques of chapter four along with basic striking techniques from Isshinryu Karate. After learning the first several movements of the system (reference chapter six), the student begins the process of putting together the sequences of the Liuhebafa form.

Start the form in a natural stance with feet should width apart and toes slightly pointed outward. The hands are open and relaxed.

Slowly bend slightly at the knees to drop your center of gravity. This is in preparation to rise upward again with your torso. At the same time, your hands begin to rise in front of you in alignment with the speed of your body rising upward.

The hands remain open and relaxed and continue to rise upward slowly (photo above and below). Your inhale is slow and deliberate through your nose. This action mirrors the breathing exercises presented earlier.

The hands continue to rise at the speed of the inhale of breath. Notice the legs are now straighter; however, a slight bend in the knees remains.

The hands continue to rise upward towards the head region. Notice the fingertips are now facing inward and do not touch.

As the hands finally reach the head region, the hands begin to circle outward. Notice the circular structure of the arms which provides all the strength needed from bone and tendon connectivity. Muscle activation is avoided. Two of the eight methods of Liuhebafa are shown above: Bone and Shape. Begin to exhale the breath at this point through the nose.

Hands continue in an outward, circular motion.

Liuhebafa | 127

The hands begin to drop downward slowly to return to your center (photo above and below). The knees begin to bend slightly as well to drop your center of gravity again. Every movement is coordinated: hands dropping, knees bending, exhale of the breath.

The photos above and below demonstrate the continuation of the hands and torso dropping as the hands come to your center. Two additional methods of the eight methods of Liuhebafa are contained in the photo sequences so far: Rise and Return.

As the hands come together, they begin to rise again toward the head region. The torso also rises along with the hands. Your inhale speed matches the hand motion and the rise in your torso.

Photos above and below show the hands rising toward the head region. Again, all speed of motion is similar to that of Tai Chi Chuan. Notice the hands remain open and relaxed at all times.

Liuhebafa

As hands reach head region, begin to lower your torso and exhale your breath. Your right hand now begins to slowly press down in front of you (photos above and below).

Your right hand extends below your waist while your left hand remains at your solar plexis area. Envision you are securing the opponent's neck and head at this point in the form.

Bring hands into a circular position with palms of both hands facing one another. Bring right hand up and outward and left hand downward towards the waist. While moving, the hands begin to rise again with your torso by straightening the legs a bit.

When the right hand rises to the shoulder area, the left hand begins to move to your right. At this point, the motions of the form resemble breathing exercise #4 presented in chapter four.

On your right side the hands switch positions and now your left hand is at your head region and your right hand slides downward and comes across your body with the palm facing upward. Envision carrying a large ball and turning your torso at the waist. Do not rely on any muscle during your movement. Again, notice the circular structure of the left arm. Focus on your breathing and moving your chi (energy) along your limbs at all times.

Photos above and below show continuation of turning your torso to your left. When the right hand extends to where it is below the left hand, raise up the right hand and turn back to your right. The right hand will come up and out in a circular motion to your right.

As your right hand comes up and outward to the right, you also rise slightly with your torso. Rising and dropping your center of gravity is a continual theme. Notice that both arms maintain the rounded structure noted previously in the form. Hands remain open and relaxed.

Continuation of the torso movement back to your right is shown above and below. When the right hand moves past your head region it begins to drop downward. Maintain a slow deliberate pace. All movements work in tandem: limbs, torso rising and falling, breathing.

Liuhebafa | 133

As the right hands drops to same level as the left hand, move both hands back to your left. Imagine moving your *chi* (energy) from side to side. Keep all muscles relaxed and rely upon the structure of your body to move. Think bones, tendons, ligaments, fascia.

Photos above and below show continuation of moving both hands back to your left. Maintain slow, deliberate pace and keep breathing through the nose.

At near full extension of both arms, turn the left palm inward and imagine controlling the opponent's arm and bringing it back to your center with both hands in front of you.

Continuation of slowly bringing both hands in front to your center. Use your waist to turn your torso and do not rely upon muscle.

Adjust your stance by bringing your left foot inward and prepare to step back outward on a 45-degree angle with the same left foot. As you are adjusting your stance, your hands come upward with the palms facing you. Keep the hands open and relaxed.

Step outward on a 45-degree angle with the left foot. Set the heel of the foot down first (gently) and bring your bodyweight forward slightly and lower your center of gravity while extending both hands outward to your sides. The hands will be on a 45-degree angle.

Adjust your stance again by bringing your right foot forward and behind your left foot. Your motion will next go towards the back and left on a 45-degree angle.

Settle the bodyweight with 60 percent on the right foot and 40 percent on the left foot. Prepare your hands by bringing the right hand in front of you with the outside edge facing the intended target/opponent. Notice hands remain open and relaxed. The arms remain bent and circular and not extended or tense in any way.

Move in slightly with the left foot into a natural stance. Extend the right hand forward for a knifehand strike to the centerline.

The series of pictures above demonstrates the opening sequences to the Liuhebafa form learned within the Chi-Ryu Jiujitsu curriculum. This is clearly meant to be an introduction only. Liuhebafa is an internal martial art that requires a deep level of introspection and continuous practice and study to grasp. This takes a considerable number of years. Liuhebafa movements incorporate minor adjustments in each movement in order for you to remain relaxed and flow in a manner similar to water. These intricacies cannot be reflected in photographs. You need to experience Liuhebafa first hand to notice such intricate movements.

The benefits of the internal martial arts such as Liuhebafa are immense and will allow you to continue training well into your advanced years. It seems the more you practice and research the form of Liuhebafa, the more you uncover and understand regarding efficiency of movement, structure, and breathing and how that can enhance your overall martial arts development.

Liuhebafa – Six Harmonies and Eight Methods

Six Harmonies (Combinations)

Body and Mind Combine

Mind and Intention Combine

Intention and Chi Combine

Chi and Spirit Combine

Spirit and Movement Combine

Movement and Emptiness Combine

Eight Methods (Principles)

Chi

Bone

Shape

Follow

Rise

Return

Retain

Conceal

FORMS OF CHI-RYU JIUJITSU

CHAPTER 8

"A prerequisite for studying a single kata is that the karate-ka take responsibility for his or her own progress."

- Master Bill Burgar

A common aspect of most martial arts systems is the learning, practicing, and internalization of prearranged sequences, or forms. These forms contain various fighting techniques and applications of defense that are important to the respective martial art you are studying. Japanese and Okinawan martial arts use the word *kata*, translated to mean "fighting form," to refer to their forms. Chinese martial arts use the term *tao lu* and Korean styles generally use the word *pumsae*. Forms, or specially devised defensive techniques against empty hands and modern-day weapons were developed specifically for Chi-Ryu Jiujitsu. For Chi-Ryu Jiujitsu, the term *forms* is preferred to the traditional karate term *kata* because it connotates the greater possibilities and applications within any movement rather than techniques that have clearly defined and, therefore, limited parameters including stopping and starting.

As C.W. Nicol explains in *Moving Zen*, "It is hard to describe kata, but once seen, the feeling they express is not forgotten. Kata are ritual battles in which the karate-ka fights several imaginary opponents. Ritual is the frame on which power and speed are built, and it is through the ritual of the kata that the karate-ka strives for perfection." He goes on to say, "Like all kata, it seems to the watcher like a strangely dynamic dance. It is beautiful to watch, for it is a battle without bloodshed or vanquished, and perhaps "dance" is a good word to link to kata."

Chi Ryu Jiujitsu places a high emphasis on the practice of forms. The necessity of forms is evident as it helps the student to more fully understand the nuances behind the techniques being learned and under practice. In addition, these forms help the student tap into the history of martial arts, the history of training and practice of his or her instructor, which in turn points back to the founders of many systems developed in China, Japan, Okinawa, and other eastern countries. As Nicol states, "I believe that when we practice kata, we are somehow touching the warrior ancestry of all humanity."

The purpose and practice of forms is intended to lead to a transformation of the state of mind of the practitioner. At first the form will be very complex and difficult to memorize; therefore, that tends to be the main focus of the mind when learning a new form. Over time, the idea is to make the various movements and techniques second in nature so then the student can start to visualize opponents and 'see' the technique working, as intended. Many refer to this as a Zen-like state of mind. This Zen state of mind requires a controlled rage, and a calmness and confidence blended with it at the same time. When this level of performance is achieved, the student must seek further and begin to 'follow through' with the mind after a technique is completed. This is evidenced by controlled breathing, seeing 'through' the opponent yet being able to take in the entire field of vision, and demonstrating that he or she could have easily continued with techniques had the need presented itself.

Students of martial arts often get lost in the outer form of the form or kata (the physical) and are not able to comprehend the internal mindfulness, feeling of energy, and appreciation of each move or technique. The internal aspects of martial arts and development of those qualities, that is the true art. This internal work is what grows as our body ages. The body and martial art is just the vehicle the person uses to find the true art and express oneself. This outer form will fade, but this internal form, lives forever.

In terms of Japanese, this frame of mind all practitioners should strive for is called *zanshin*. "Zan" means to remain in the moment, to continue. "Shin" means heart or mind. So the essence of zanshin is to maintain proper awareness of body and mind and not relaxing your spirit. Training the internal aspects of the martial arts, as is done with Liuhebafa practice included within Chi-Ryu Jiujitsu, is a critical element of training to relax your spirit. Nicol recalls in his book *Moving Zen* the time his sensei explained this to him, "Kata is not just a practice of movements, and neither is it a way of retreating into your own self. When you practice kata you must be acutely aware. You must have a mind like still water, reflecting all things. Finish your kata with zanshin, otherwise, no matter how brilliantly you perform it, it will be considered a failure."

Stances are critically important for sound understanding and performance of the forms within Chi-Ryu Jiujitsu. Stances or stances in general should be 'non-static,' but constantly free flowing to facilitate all techniques with maximum energy. This runs a bit counterintuitive to stances within karate styles of training where stances tend to be more static, a bit elongated with emphasis and exertion of leg muscles to form a strong position to deliver a punch or kick. At more advanced stages, the karate-ka begins to emphasize the flowing aspects of stances; however, Chi-Ryu Jiujitsu looks to begin this process sooner as extremely hard punching and kicking is not necessary for a close range technique to be effective.

A YouTube video called *3 Kata Secrets* by Iain Abernethy and Jesse Enkamp explores the aspects of stances on the execution of karate kata. They note in the video that if your body moves in a combative situation the same as it does when you perform kata, you will be easily overrun by your opponent. The skill can only be effective when the body is utilizing transitional, or non-static postures or in the transition aspects of your movement combined with the application of the technique. Far too often, martial artists begin this exploration of stances, movement, and application of technique only after many years of training in rigid stances and postures. The forms of Chi-Ryu Jiujitsu aim to remove such stances and get the student moving in coordination with their defense applications to create structurally sound and natural movements that can be immediately applied, when needed.

Chi-Ryu Jiujitsu has nine forms within the system. They are listed below followed by the person who developed the form:

1. Waking Hands Form / Grandmaster Latimer
2. Circle Form / Grandmaster Latimer
3. Raking Fist Form / Grandmaster Latimer
4. Brooklyn 819 / Grandmaster Latimer
5. Breaking Waves Form / Master Costanzo
6. Silver Shadow Form / Master Costanzo
7. Sleeping Dragon Form / Master McDonald
8. Waking Dragon Form (Arnis stick) / Master McDonald
9. Raging Dragon Form (short staff) / Master McDonald

Also included in the forms curriculum for Chi-Ryu Jiujitsu is the Liuhebafa form discussed in the previous chapter where the initial movements are demonstrated. Three of the nine forms are presented in the following chapters: Raking Fist Form, Breaking Waves Form, and Waking Dragon Form.

RAKING FIST FORM

CHAPTER 9

As the developer of the Raking Fist form, Grandmaster Latimer's purpose was to establish the concept of chambering where the hands are and to formerly introduce the raking fist technique as a viable self-defense tool. The raking fist is utilized from an elevated position of either hand relative to the opponent's head from his standing posture. It takes on the angle of 45 degrees and targets most frequently the temple, eye, and bridge of the opponent's nose.

Raking fist technique is a continuous movement along the face mask area and intensifies the level of pain the opponent experiences by the elongation of surface wound area and speed at which the major knuckles of the fist rake across the targeted areas. The elevation of force in the technique is created by the motion of the body dropping and torquing in the direction of the movement of the raking fist.

Targeting the temple area of an opponent will cause loss of balance, sudden overall loss of physical awareness, panic, and inability to be competently combative or purposeful. The movement across the opponent's eyes will have the effect of distorting his vision and increase the pain level to the eyes and body in general. Lastly, the continued raking movement of the fist across the bridge of the nose will further increase the level of pain the attacker experiences and sends him into a surrender mindset and desire to have the points of contact with this particular strike to end suddenly.

For the right-handed person utilizing this technique with the right hand and at a 45 degree angle as described here is very much like the number one strike in the martial art of Modern Arnis. The contact point would be the left temple of an opponent.

The added use for the raking fist strike is what Grandmaster Latimer calls the *hooking raking fist* and is equally as devastating and useful as the traditional raking fist strike. The manner of execution in the hooking raking fist is such that an opponent would have difficulty in determining the pattern of movement from its genesis throughout the mid-range path and its point of impact. This strike, though similar in basic strategy to that of the conventional hook punch in boxing, is not a basic circular movement or attack with the fist. This strike essentially has at least two paths to its delivery movement.

The hooking raking fist combines a circular movement that elongates into a near horizontal line of attack and then reverts back to a circular movement. This movement creates an illusion as to where it is coming from, how fast it is traveling and, most importantly, where is it intended to impact the attacker. Much like the conventional hook punch it can be targeted and directed to the body and head. Unlike the conventional hook punch, in boxing and other fighting arts, this technique maintains the same attitude and purpose as the normal raking fist strike of Chi-Ryu Jiujitsu which is to slash and rake the surface area of the intended target. The striking fist in this case will be turned to the target at the last second by a whipping of the wrist and the torquing of the body to the target area on the opponent. The target will most often be the same as in the raking fist technique with the contact primarily focused to the temple and eyes. The knuckles of the striking fist in this case will be primarily facing the opponent's head with the thumb of the hand facing downward upon impact. The follow through of the striking fist is a continuous and fast, slashing type movement.

Here again, this striking method is very similar to a movement in the martial art of Modern Arnis utilizing the stick or baston. The advantage of this strike as it is performed in Chi-Ryu Jiujitsu is that it is very much like the Arnis movement called *dobleede doblada*. In this Arnis movement, the stick is twirled in a small circle into a big circular strike in a downward motion. This double spin could be a double strike or a block followed up with a strike in one smooth, flowing movement. In the striking method of Chi-Ryu Jiujitsu, this strike would be targeted to the head or facial area as the knuckles of the striking fist would first be delivered with the thumb knuckle downward. The rotation to the downward large circular strike would be performed with the knuckles of the same fist rotated and facing upward.

The Raking Fist form also includes movement #9 from the 30 movements that Chi-Ryu Jiujitsu teaches. Finally, Raking Fist includes liberal usage of arm control techniques to allow you to conduct close-range striking counters. For those with prior martial arts experience it is easy to utilize too much muscular power during the performance of this form. You need to remember the concepts presented in the chapters on breathing and the MiXXiNG drill.

Let your skeletal structure and the tendons and fascia handle the movement of your techniques. Your breathing must be deliberate and controlled as well in order to gain the most efficiency out of your overall performance. The minute you rely upon muscle and strength during Raking Fist or any of the Chi-Ryu Jiujitsu forms for that matter, you will have a tendency to tense up and get locked into an unwanted posture or situation, and your reaction time will dimmish substantially.

Raking Fist Form | 147

> Please note that due to the fluid nature of the motions involved with Chi-Ryu Jiujitsu forms, it is difficult to capture every motion and every little detail. Some of the sequences presented may actually jump over a motion or two in order to present the material in the best possible manner. The author accepts full responsibility for any errors and omissions.

Attention stance stepping into relaxed ready posture with hands open.

Perform block to head region to defend attacker's roundhouse punch. Do not use muscle but rather rely upon the body's natural structure to stop the attack. Immediately control the attacker's punching arm with an outside-in circular motion. Perform upper cut punch to attacker's center mass.

With the same hand you punched with, perform palm heel strike to attacker's shoulder region to further disorient the attacker's balance. Control with a grab immediately after the palm strike and execute front kick to attacker's groin region.

Conclusion of the front kick to attacker's groin region.

CLOSE-UP DEPICTION OF LAST THREE TECHNIQUES

The palm heel strike that immediately follows the upper cut punch. Intention is to further disorient the attacker's balance in order to control for the grab and front kick.

The palm heel strike to the attacker's shoulder is immediately followed by a grab at the same area to control the attacker.

Front kick to attacker's groin region. Notice the defender is striking with the shin bone rather than using the ball of the foot utilized most often in traditional karate techniques. Note that many street defense engagements may not allow you to utilize traditional techniques.

The front kick is immediately followed with a ridgehand strike to attacker's neck region.

Control opponent's head and immediately execute an elbow strike to attacker's head region.

Lift attacker's head and prepare your right arm for the raking fist strike.

The raking fist strike travels along a right to left plane across attacker's head region. The fist must turn inward so the knuckles of the pointer and middle finger connect with the target. Shuffle inward slightly and perform an elbow strike with the right arm.

Immediately follow up with a knife hand strike with the same arm as the elbow strike. Control with your right hand and execute a palm heel strike to attacker's head region.

Both hands now control by grabbing attacker's clothing. Execute a takedown to the left on a 45-degree angle. Follow with a stomping kick with the right foot (not shown).

Pivot and turn back to the front and execute inside deflection block with your left arm.

After a knife hand strike to attacker's throat region immediately after the inside deflection, control attacker's arm and perform a kick to attacker's knee.

Maintaining control over attacker's right arm, perform another palm heel strike to attacker's shoulder region as shown previously. Follow up with a stomping-type kick with our right foot to opponent's knee.

Raking Fist Form | 155

Set down your foot and execute a open backhand strike and immediately follow with a knifehand strike.

CLOSE-UP DEPICTION OF LAST THREE TECHNIQUES

After the palm heel strike with your right hand to attacker's shoulder, control the attacker's position and perform a stomping kick with your right foot to inside of attacker's knee.

After the stomping kick, set your foot down inward toward opponent. Notice control over the opponent's left arm is maintained. Execute an open backhand strike to attacker's midsection or rib area.

Remain relaxed and fluid in your movement so you are able to bounce back from the open backhand strike into an immediate knifehand strike to the same region. This is a fluid, non-stop double tap type of striking sequence.

After the double tap strike to attacker's ribs, execute a sweeping circular motion with right arm to perform a takedown (your right foot must be between attacker's feet for the trip out). Now attacker attempts a roundhouse punch coming in from left angle. Perform head block and keep circular structure of your left arm to defend.

This sequence follows movement #9 from the 30 total movements. Your right arm performs a hammer fist strike to attacker's elbow/forearm region. Continue this fluid motion and bring attacker's arm to the inside and circle your right arm under and around attacker's arm to control.

Your left hand performs a palm strike to attacker's head and your left arm immediately comes down with elbow strike onto attacker's arm to move it back to the left. This clears space for your right hand to immediately follow with a claw strike to attacker's throat and then follow with a palm strike to attacker's chin. Follow with a step through with your right foot and perform a takedown.

New attacker grabs your left shoulder. Trap their hand with your right hand and turn inward while maintaining control over their hand on your shoulder.

Wrap your left arm around attacker's arm for control and execute uppercut punch. Step to rear with your left foot and perform a takedown with circular motion of your right arm.

New attacker attempts a roundhouse style kick. Stabilize your stance and bring both arms in front in a relaxed manner. Do not use muscle to block. Allow structure of the position to handle the defense. Immediately control attacker's foot and execute downward elbow to attacker's foot/ankle.

Chi-Ryu Jiujitsu

After the downward elbow strike, reach over and grab attacker's foot. Turn slightly to the front to unbalance attacker further and twist foot in order for a takedown.

Turn to your right to face new attacker and deflect their punch to the outside with your right hand. Do not rely upon strength to deflect the punch which allows for an immediate knifehand strike with the blocking arm (shown next).

After knifehand strike, retract your right hand and pull attacker's arm in for an immediate knifehand strike with your left hand.

Execute a knee kick with your left foot. Continue the forward motion by executing a double knifehand strike to attacker's shoulder region.

Maintain calm posture and controlled breathing while looking back across the area of attack for any other threat. Step inward into a guarded posture and conclude by stepping forward with your right foot to conduct formal ending bow.

BREAKING WAVES FORM

CHAPTER 10

The Breaking Waves form, developed by Master John Costanzo, is mainly inspired from the training and defense concepts initiated by Grandmaster Latimer. Chi-Ryu Jiujitsu training can adapt to each student's physical attributes and tendencies. Movements #8 and #18 are front and center within Breaking Waves form along with inspirations from the Liuhebafa form. Master Costanzo notes, "I was intrigued by Chi-Ryu Jiujitsu's phrase *one thing moves, everything moves*, and devised different sequences highlighting fluidity of motion."

Breaking Waves incorporates blocking the opponents attack, engaging, using grappling controls, striking vulnerable areas, changing angles of defense and ultimately clearing the attacker away from the combat. All these concepts are performed with a flow of movement by manipulating the attacker's moves against them. The motions are meant to resemble waves pounding on the shore, as the circular overhead ridge hand strikes to the back of the neck demonstrate.

The initial attention stance and courtesy bow associated with all forms performed in martial arts.

Stepping forward with left foot and preparing the hands in a relaxed manner keeping them open so as to have the ability to react naturally. Opponent attempts a grab to the front. Slide forward slightly with left foot to close the gap. Spring forward with slight body drop on this motion and throw your entire body into the motion. Parry the opponent's hands outward. The genesis of this technique derives from breathing exercise #2 in chapter 4.

Note: This opening sequence is presented in the Movements chapter (movement #8). The left hand projects straight to the opponent's chin area for a strike. The right hand parries arm outward and continues in a circular manner from high to low in order to execute a strike to opponent's groin area.

The circular motion of the right arm is completed all while controlling opponent's other arm after the chin strike with the left hand. After the right hand strike (inside of hand called a ridge hand), grab whatever is available to pull opponent into a left elbow strike to the side of their head region.

Elbow strike is completed and same arm executes a knifehand strike to the neck area.

Continue with an overhead ridge hand strike to opponent's back of neck region. Your body should rise slightly and then drop on the strike.

Control opponent's head after the prior strike and execute elbow strike to the head. Left hand turns opponent's chin inward while right hand controls the shoulder region so opponent cannot stand up. This motion guides the opponent to your center region for greater control.

Turn opponent's head inward and quickly turn his head back to the outside while simultaneously stepping in same direction with the left foot. This clears opponent out of the way on a 90-degree angle. The torquing motion of your body to the left enhances the effectiveness of the motion.

Block new attack to the front and with same hand strike to opponent's neck region with open hand knifehand.

Completion of the knifehand strike to the neck region. Shuffle closer to opponent and execute a body check technique with an open hand backhand and a knifehand strike to opponent's floating ribs area.

After the body check, pick up an opponent with your peripheral vision attempting a choke on your right side. Protect your head region and prevent the choke with the reaction of raising your right arm. Execute elbow strike to the rear with your left arm.

Breaking Waves Form | 171

Turn and clear out attacker's left arm who previously tried the choke hold. Clear their arm out of the way and immediately follow with an overhand strike.

Lift attacker's head slightly to disorient and unbalance the attacker further and execute a knee strike.

Clear the attacker away from you by whipping your left arm towards the rear and stepping to the rear with your left foot (note: the sequence is meant to face the opposite side of the beginning of the form so these angles are reversed).

Step in with right foot and begin a circular parry with both hands against opponent's right front grab or punch. Immediately follow the parry with a straight punch to the midsection.

After the punch, follow with a knifehand strike to the throat and immediately control with a hook (called a yoke) with the same striking hand.

Complete the yoke by driving your forearm into attacker's throat and follow with a knee strike to opponent's lower back region.

Complete this sequence with a downward elbow strike to opponent's solar plexis region.

CLOSE-UP DEPICTION OF LAST SERIES OF TECHNIQUES

Opponent attempts a front grab or punch.

Breaking Waves Form | 175

Bring both hands up in a circular parry motion from your left to your right (outside to inside).

Complete the circular parry and control at the wrist with your left hand.

Follow with a punch to the solar plexis region.

Switch hands: Bring your right hand back to control opponent's arm and simultaneously execute a knifehand strike to opponent's neck area. The follow through is essential at this point to perform the hooking control shown next.

Fingers hook opponent's neck while the left arm bends allowing the forearm to clamp into opponent's neck.

Execute knee strike to lower back of opponent.

Complete the sequence with a downward elbow strike to opponent's solar plexis region.

Turning back to the front, deflect opponent's front grab. Maintain a circular posture with the arms. Immediately close the gap by shuffling forward and execute a double knifehand strike to opponent's neck region.

Breaking Waves Form | 179

Control opponent's arm or shoulder area with your right hand and execute palm strike to opponent's opposite shoulder to disorient and unbalance him.

Immediately control opponent's head by securing the neck with left hand and pull into your shoulder area.

Adjust your hand positioning by bringing your right hand under opponent's tricep region of their left arm and push away. Note: while you push with right hand bring attacker's left arm upward, your left hand is pressing downward on attacker's head. The up and down motions of your hands along with your body torquing to the left sends attacker to the floor.

Come back to the front in ready posture with hands open and relaxed. Finish with courtesy bow by stepping up with your right foot to your left.

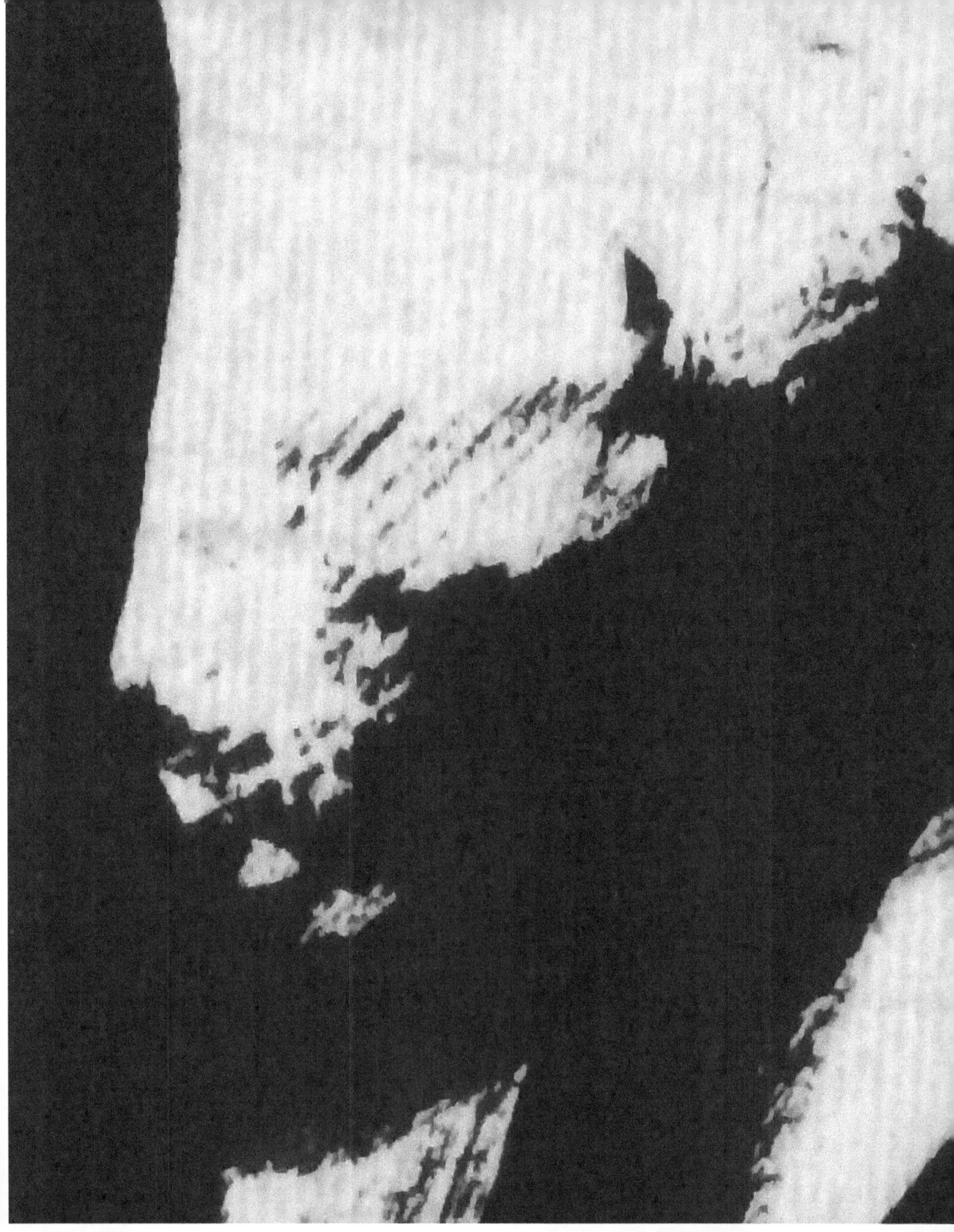

WAKING DRAGON FORM

CHAPTER 11

Developed by Master John McDonald, the Waking Dragon form adds stick fighting into the Chi-Ryu Jiujitsu requirements. Basic strikes from Modern Arnis along with neck and arm locks are the essential concepts contained in Waking Dragon. The techniques from this form can apply to a stick, cane, umbrella and so on. Chi-Ryu Jiujitsu includes training in Modern Arnis, so the student will get familiar with practical weapons such as stick and knife instead of traditional weapons found in traditional budo systems of martial arts.

With reverse grip on stick, prepare to step forward with your right foot.

Swing the stick from right to left and catch under your left arm. This is a non-aggressive posture with your weapon yet you remain poised to react when needed.

Attacker attempts a front stab with a knife. Adjust your stance to the outside and lower your stick for a strike to the top of attacker's wrist or forearm.

Waking Dragon Form | 185

Shuffle forward and strike attacker under the chin or neck region, whichever presents itself.

Follow with a strike to attacker's neck region with the end of your stick. Quickly turn your stick over (palm down on the prior strike to palm up) in order to begin a neck lock leading to a takedown.

With your stick now behind attacker's neck, step around and back with your left foot and bring the tip of your stick downward leading to a neck lock and potential takedown.

Finishing posture of the neck lock (NOTE: close up photos of this sequence at the end).

Continue against new attacker with a figure eight sequence starting with the left hand.

Switch hands and repeat the figure eight with the right hand.

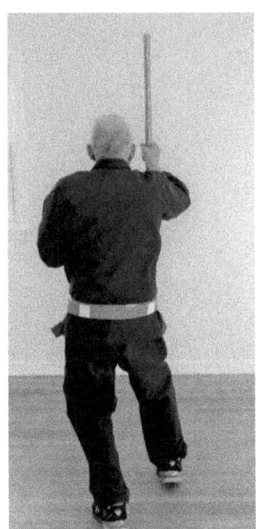

Conclude the sequence with an overhead strike (strike #12 from Modern Arnis).

Turn back to the front to face a new attacker and block an overhead strike with your stick. Immediately deflect the strike to the outside.

Grab attacker's wrist (right arm) and immediately execute front snapping kick to groin region (or knee region) with left foot.

Landing forward with your left kicking foot to gain additional inside space, execute a thrust strike with the bottom of your stick to floating rib area of attacker. Immediately tuck your stick under opponent's right arm (NOTE: you still control wrist of the right arm) and begin turning toward the rear to execute an arm lock and takedown.

Complete the step and turn to the rear to execute the arm lock and takedown.

New attacker comes from your left with a knife stab. Turn and strike downward with both hands.

After striking on top of attacker's arm, continue motion upward to clear attacker's arm out of the way.

Once arm is cleared, continue to bring your stick around attacker's neck to perform a neck lock and takedown.

With stick around back of attacker's neck, secure attacker's head with your left hand against your stick. Begin to step backward and torque to the front with your left foot for the takedown.

Finish the takedown technique to the front and check your left flank for any potential attack.

Waking Dragon Form | 193

Continue and check your right flank for any potential attack. With no other threat, step forward and conclude with a formal bow.

CLOSE-UP DEPICTION OF OPENING SEQUENCE OF WAKING DRAGON

Your posture is non-aggressive yet you have a capability to react quickly.

Attacker attempts knife stab. Adjusting your stance off the centerline of the stab, bring your stick downward to strike attacker's wrist area.

Shuffle inward immediately to strike upward and under attacker's chin.

Waking Dragon Form | 195

Continue with a strike to attacker's face or neck region with bottom of your stick.

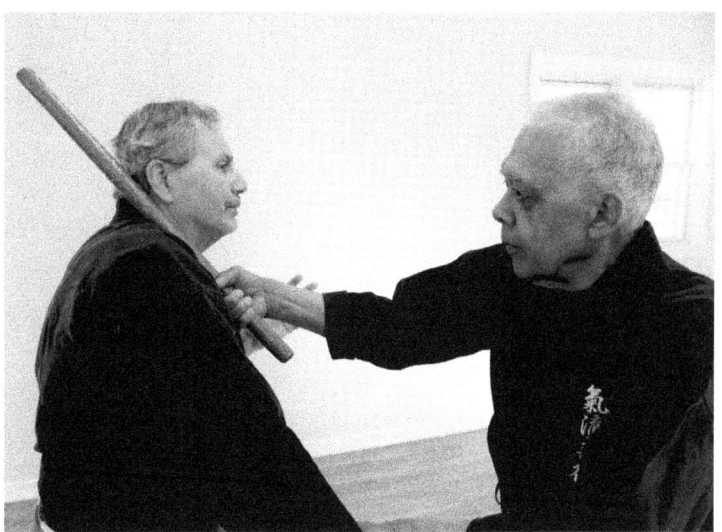

Follow through with a strike to attacker's neck area which sets up a neck lock with your weapon.

Turn your stick over while maintaining contact with attacker.

Circle your stick around the back of attacker's neck and bring your left hand up to grab the top of your stick to lock attacker's neck.

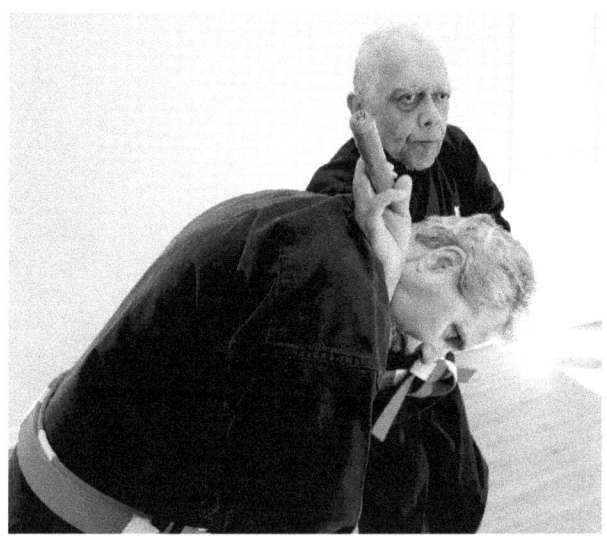

Stepping back and away, bring your left hand down to crank the attacker's neck and for a potential takedown.

APPENDIX

PHOTO CREDITS

All photos taken by the author, Dan Popp, except as otherwise noted below.

Chapter 1

Description	Credit
Grandmaster Isham Latimer – painting example	Isham Latimer
Grandmaster Isham Latimer – fighting stance	Isham Latimer
Group photo including Sensei Malachi Lee	Isham Latimer
Master John Costanzo in Vietnam	Isham Latimer
Master John Costanzo – graphic design /illustration example	Isham Latimer
New York Times review of Split Second	Isham Latimer
Master John McDonald – Order of Isshin-Ryu black belt promotion	Isham Latimer

Chapter 2

Description	Credit
Grandmaster Walter 'Toby' Cooling Tribute	Greg LeBlanc
Modern Arnis Certificate	John McDonald
Modern Arnis Training Plan/ Notes	Isham Latimer

Chapter 4

Description	Credit
Group Photo at park (Hugh/ McDonald/ Latimer/ Costanzo)	Isham Latimer

SOURCES

Book Sources

5 Rules for White Belts, by Chris Matakas - ©2020 by Chris Matakas. Published by Ferryman Services, Inc.

Aikido for Life, by Gaku Homma - ©1990 by Gaku Homma. Published by North Atlantic Books.

Breath, by James Nestor - ©2020 by James Nestor. Published by Riverhead Books (Penguin Random House LLC).

Breathe – A Life in Flow, by Rickson Gracie - ©2021 by Rickson Gracie. Published by HarperCollins.

Courage is Calling, by Ryan Holiday - ©2021 by Ryan Holiday. Published by Penguin Random House LLC.

Five Years One Kata. Putting Kata Back at the Heart of Karate, by Bill Burgar - ©2003 William Burgar. Published by Martial Arts Publishing Limited.

Karate – My Life, by Kanazawa Hirokazu – translated by Alex Bennett - ©2003 Kendo World Publications Ltd. (English edition)

Liuhebafa Five Character Secrets, by Paul Dillon - ©2003 by Paul Dillon. YMAA Publication Center, Inc.

Mindful Running, by Mackenzie L. Havey - ©2017 Mackenzie L. Havey. Published by Bloomsbury Publishing Plc.

Modern Day Warriors: In Their Own Words, Vol. 2, by Cleveland Robinson - ©Cleveland Robinson. Lulu.com (ID: 18158861)

Moving Zen: Karate as a Way to Gentleness, by C.W. Nicol - ©2018 C.W. Nicol

Natural Born Heroes, by Christopher McDougall - ©2015 by Christopher McDougall. Published by Alfred A. Knopf, a division of Random House LLC, New York.

On Jiu Jitsu, by Chris Matakas - ©2017 by Chris Matakas. Published by Build the Fire Publishing.

Order of Isshin-Ryu: One Family, One Dojo, by Dan Popp - ©2018 by Dan Popp. Published by Kamel Press, LLC.

Shaolin Chin Na, The Seizing Art of Kung-Fu, by Yang Jwing-Ming - ©1980 Unique Publications, Inc.

T'ai Chi Ch'uan and I Ching, by Da Liu - ©1972 by Da Liu. Harper & Row, Publishers.

The Bible of Karate – Bubishi, translated with commentary by Patrick McCarthy - ©1995 by Patrick McCarthy. Published by the Charles E. Tuttle Company, Inc.

The Five Word Poem of LiuHeBaFa, by Hui Kit Wah, Stuart Agars, and Ruth Hampson – 01 March 2021. Self-published.

The Power of Positive Thinking, by Norman Vincent Peale - ©1952, 1956 by Prentic-Hall, Inc. Copyright renewed ©1980 by Norman Vincent Peale. Published by Touchstone, A Division of Simon & Schuster, Inc.

The Wim Hof Method, by Wim Hof - ©2020 by Wim Hof. Published by Sounds True, Inc.

Internet Sources

Google searches and internet sources provided historical photographs, articles and maps presented in this text.

Chi-Ryu Jiujitsu

www.wakinghands.com

Cleveland Clinic

https://my.clevelandclinic.org/health/articles/9445-diaphragmatic-breathing

Harvard Health Publishing

https://www.health.harvard.edu/lung-health-and-disease/learning-diaphragmatic-breathing

International Isshinryu Hall of Fame

https://www.theihof.com/1980-1990

Jujutsu (Wikipedia)

https://en.wikipedia.org/wiki/Jujutsu

Koguma West Goju-Ryu

http://www.kogumawest.com/master-taganashi-and

Liuhebafa

A Brief Discussion of Liu He Ba Fa, by Xiaoling Liu

http://www.wudanglongmen.com/liuhebafa.html

Liuhebafa Chuan – The 4th Internal Art, written by Nomura Akihiko

HIDEN Budo & Bujutsu

Sanuces-Ryu

https://en.wikipedia.org/wiki/Moses_Powell

Sanuces Ryu Jujutsu

https://www.tetsunami.com/tetsunami-jujutsu/sanuces-ryu/

Seiryoku-Zenyo

http://kodokanjudoinstitute.org/en/doctrine/word/seiryoku-zenyo/

Shaffer's Red Dragon Street Defense

https://www.facebook.com/Shaffers-Red-Dragon-Street-Defense-227069464101913/

The Way of Seiryoku Zenyo – Jita Kyoei in Judo

By Shinichi Oimatsu

https://judoinfo.com/seiryoku2/

The Wall Street Journal. The Healing Power of Proper Breathing, by James Nestor. May 21, 2020.

Internet Images

Moses Powell (1941 – 2005)
https://www.pinterest.ph/pin/80150068338802468/

Remy Presas (1936 – 2001)
https://www.google.com/search?q=Remy+Presas&rlz=1C1CHBF_

YouTube

3 Kata Secrets. By Iain Abernethy and Jesse Enkamp.

ABOUT THE AUTHOR

Dan began the study of Isshinryu Karate in 1982. Currently holding the rank of hachi-dan (8th degree black belt), Dan was named the 2008 Male Instructor of the Year by the International Isshinryu Hall of Fame and subsequently inducted into the Isshinryu Hall of Fame in July 2013. He has served on the Board of Directors for the Order of Isshin-Ryu, founded by Grandmaster Toby Cooling in 1971. Dan's training in martial arts also includes Modern Arnis and Kombatan. He is a student of these stick fighting arts originating in the Philippines under the direction of Grandmaster Rick Manglinong, where he currently holds the rank of Lakan Apat (4th degree black belt) in SMP Arnis. For the past thirteen years, Dan has been a formal student of Chi-Ryu Jiujitsu training directly with the founders: Grandmaster Isham Latimer, Master John Costanzo and Master John McDonald. He was elevated to san-dan (3rd degree black belt) in Chi-Ryu Jiujitsu in April 2023.

In 1990, Dan began his study of Kendo under Sensei Duk Yeong Kim, progressing to the rank of yon-dan (4th degree black belt). In tandem with Kendo, Sensei Kim provided Dan instruction in the art of Shodo or Japanese calligraphy. Although his Kendo/Shodo sensei passed away in 2007, Dan continues to practice Shodo to honor his teacher. Dan's works have been exhibited at Mulberry Art Studios in Lancaster, PA and at Gallery at Second in Harrisburg, PA. Nationally his commissioned works can be found in Arizona, California, Delaware, Florida, Georgia, Nevada, Oregon, Puerto Rico, Texas, and Virginia. His international commissions include Australia and Canada. Dan has recently started combining the traditional aspects of Shodo by introducing acrylics on larger canvases to expand the possibilities of his art. He is also branching out into abstract subjects with emphasis on building texture into his work.

He is the author of four books which can be ordered through Amazon or direct from the publisher in both print and Kindle: *Sensei's Final Lessons – A Memoir*, published 2012 by Outskirts Press, *The Floating Brush: Learning Japanese Calligraphy from a Kendo Master*, published 2014 by Kamel Press, *Order of Isshin Ryu – One Family, One Dojo*, published 2018 *by Kamel Press, and Essence of Reflection,* published in 2021 by Kamel Press.

A 1994 graduate of The Pennsylvania State University with a B.S. in Professional Accountancy, Dan was employed in 1999 by the National Credit Union Administration where he still serves as a federal examiner specializing in IT audits. He holds several IT and information security audit certifications including CISA, CGEIT, and CRISC. He resides in Harrisburg, PA with his two daughters, Britteni and Kayla.

www.ingramcontent.com/pod-product-compliance
Lightning Source LLC
Chambersburg PA
CBHW060941170426
43195CB00026B/2994